GREAT MARQUES

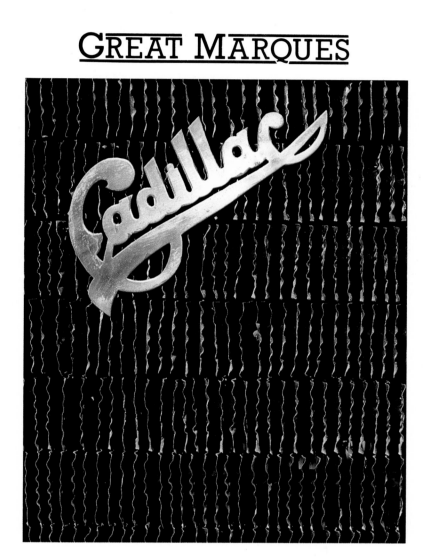

GREAT MARQUES
CADILLAC

Andrew Whyte

GENERAL EDITOR
John Blunsden

CHARTWELL
BOOKS, INC.

This edition 1989

Published by Chartwell Books, Inc.
A division of Book Sales, Inc.
110 Enterprise Avenue
Secaucus, New Jersey 07094

© Octopus Books Ltd 1986

ISBN: 1-55521-422-3

Produced by Mandarin Offset
Printed and bound in Hong Kong

Special photography in
The United States of America
by John Lamm and Dennis Adler
(see page 80 for detail)

Endpapers and pages 2–3: details
of the 1935 V12-engined series
370D Town Car for seven
passengers, provided by Jack
Frank
Page 1: radiator grille of the 1909
Demi-Tonneau, provided by Jerry
Ray Nickel
This page: chrome detail of the
1955 Cadillac Series 60 special,
provided by Frank Ormonde

CONTENTS

SETTING
THE
STANDARD

Among America's automobile names, that of Cadillac stands for quality, pure and simple – as Rolls-Royce does for Britain.

From relatively early on in its progress, the Cadillac company of Detroit, Michigan, was a division of the General Motors Corporation. It was always one of the most influential, and today Cadillac remains the jewel in the crown of GM – still probably the biggest of all employers with well over 600,000 people on its payrolls around the world. The image of quality that pervades this vast corporation can be directly attributed to the Cadillac marque – or, rather, to its creator.

The quality built into the original Cadillacs was not a matter of subjective assessment, but was proved objectively on many occasions. It was based on the need to standardize all components and their dimensions within rigid tolerances. This standardization, constantly monitored, resulted in the production of outstanding automobiles in unheard-of quantities *and* at reasonable prices.

The Cadillac possesses the longest pedigree of all the great marques of America. Most of these marques met their end as a direct or indirect result of the Wall Street crash, and maybe because they did not have the fine combination of technical and financial control that two men – Henry Martyn Leland and his son Wilfred – applied to the Cadillac.

Henry Leland's story, and therefore Cadillac's, begins even before the American Civil War.

The Leland legend unfolds

The Leland family had been established as New Englanders for nearly two centuries when Zilpha, wife of Leander Leland, gave birth to her eighth child, Henry, at Barton, Vermont, on February 16, 1843.

Pride and respectability competed with a degree of poverty at the family farm, and each member had to put his or her shoulder to the wheel. The eighth young Leland took on subcontract work for a local shoe factory. His was the simple but tedious task of fitting soles – until he devised a scheme for doing the job quicker, but just as effectively. There were no complaints from the factory and, as he was on piecework, Henry

Martyn Leland, then aged eleven, was able to earn good money.

Later the Lelands moved back to Massachusetts, their original territory, and Henry, by now aged fourteen, became a trainee at the Worcester loom works of Crompton & Knowles. He was just eighteen and too young to join the army when the war began. He admired the new president, Abraham Lincoln, and wanted to fight for the Union against the Confederacy; but it was not to be. Instead, he became an integral part of the Crompton & Knowles war effort, for many of his older colleagues were joining the colors. As top apprentice, he was put in charge of making, setting up and operating a copying lathe for the Springfield rifle works, Connecticut, and he stayed on there – only to be made redundant when peace came in the spring of 1865. The talented twenty-two-year-old Leland was snapped up by the more experienced Colt company of Hartford, Connecticut, as a skilled toolmaker.

Colt was one of the first American companies to apply the "spare parts" principle diligently: parts produced to the same specification were machined so accurately that they were identical and therefore interchangeable. Indeed such was the accuracy that could be achieved, once all the costly machine tools were in operation, that the role of the traditional craftsman, who had devoted his life to achieving near perfection by the skill of his hands, looked threatened. Two years' experience with the Colt company strengthened Leland's resolve to develop ultraefficient manufacturing techniques that were honest and true, resulting in a long-lasting product. His indigent upbringing also made it second nature for him to be concerned about the human element, believing that technical advances should not be achieved to the detriment of the individual, but put to his or her advantage.

From 1872, after several other jobs, Leland put his ever-growing experience at the disposal of the already highly reputable Brown & Sharpe engineering company. There, in Providence, Rhode Island, his career blossomed. In 1876 he created the prototype universal grinder, and perfected it over the ensuing decade. In the meantime, he set himself the task of improving efficiency in the production of sewing machines.

PREVIOUS PAGES The closed bodywork on this single-cylinder Cadillac Model E Coupe is of the type later known as the "doctor's coupe." It is among the earliest of its kind.

ABOVE Confident, prophetic words of wisdom for the early sellers.

LEFT Henry Martyn Leland, father of both Cadillac and Lincoln, photographed soon after forming the Cadillac Automobile Company. Together with his son and right-hand man Wilfred, he set special quality standards for the marque, and made sure that Cadillac provided a stable base upon which General Motors could be built.

RIGHT An early Cadillac, circa 1903, and (INSET) a contemporary competition scene. Like Rolls-Royce, however, Cadillac tended to eschew competitive events as tools of marketing.

Using his "get-it-right-first-time" principle, he bumped productivity up by nearly 50 percent within a year.

Wishing to expand its business, and noting the untapped industrial potential beyond the Appalachian Mountains, the Brown & Sharpe directorate gave Leland a roving commission to obtain orders. His special abilities enabled him to prove himself across the land, for, like all the best salesmen, he was as good as his word, winning contracts through the demonstrated accuracy of his own work.

First contacts with the automobile industry

Henry Leland was forty-seven and prosperous when the opportunity came for him to become his own master. Realizing that his mind was made up, Brown & Sharpe actually loaned him $2000 as a token of appreciation. He himself put in $1600. What got his new enterprise off the ground, however, was the sum of $40,000 provided by timber tycoon Robert Faulconer.

The year was 1890. The automobile had reached a crucial stage of its development. The internal combustion engine was known to be a practical proposition and somewhat ahead of the automobile concept itself. Most closely approaching the commercial manufacture of cars at that time were Panhard and Peugeot in France – but, everywhere in the industrialized world, the idea of mechanized personal transportation was catching on fast.

In America, which did not yet have a road system on a par with that of France, there were numerous ideas for the motive power of the future, and several men were on the verge of running their first gasoline-engined motor vehicles: notably John W. Lambert of Anderson, Indiana, who was making his first three-wheeler, and the brothers Charles E. and J. Frank Duryea of Springfield, Massachusetts, soon to get their four-wheeled buggy in motion. Although still working with steam, as were so many pioneers, Ransom Eli Olds of Lansing, Michigan, was on the point of producing *his* first practical road vehicle, too.

Initially, the Leland & Faulconer company combined precision tool and machine manufacture with an engineering consultancy – mainly to the bicycle industry, for which many thousands of fine-limit gears and other components were produced. Soon it had its own foundry, a model of its kind. Faulconer was, at one stage, worried by his partner's uncompromising nature, which led to the scrapping of many parts not quite made to the specified tolerance. Some late deliveries occurred, but the quality of goods sold was never allowed to drop and, it would seem, orders continued to pour in. Prosperity reigned.

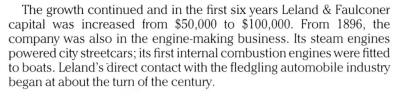

The growth continued and in the first six years Leland & Faulconer capital was increased from $50,000 to $100,000. From 1896, the company was also in the engine-making business. Its steam engines powered city streetcars; its first internal combustion engines were fitted to boats. Leland's direct contact with the fledgling automobile industry began at about the turn of the century.

Leland and the Detroit Automobile Company

R. E. Olds was about to become the world's first mass producer with his famous curved-dash runabout. What made this vehicle so smooth on the road – despite the use of a single, large cylinder – was Olds's acceptance of Leland advice and Leland technology. Soon Leland & Faulconer was producing transmission parts for the "Merry Oldsmobile," as it was dubbed. The next stage was a contract, shared with the Dodge brothers, John F. and Horace, to make engines for Olds. It is said that, in a bench test, the Leland engine was found to be nearly 20 percent more powerful than the Dodge, simply because it was made to such strict tolerances.

In the meantime, would-be car makers were proliferating, among them a group led by William Murphy. He had formed the Detroit Automobile Company in 1899. Despite the confident title, no cars were produced in the first two years. Then the superintendent of the Detroit Edison Company was recruited. That is to say he *would* have been superintendent, had he agreed to give up his experiments with cars and engines. "I had to choose between my job and my automobile," he wrote more than 20 years later. The name of the man who chose the automobile was Henry Ford, then aged thirty-seven.

It proved a bad move. This was Ford's subsequent view: "We continued making cars more or less on the model of my first car. We sold very few of them; I could get no support at all toward making better cars . . . the new company was not a vehicle for realizing my ideas but merely a money-making concern – that did not make much money. In March 1902 I resigned, determined never again to put myself under orders." (In 1903 came the first Ford series production car. In 1908 the

F.S.Bennett was responsible for the Cadillac's early success in Britain, largely through gaining the Dewar Trophy for the marque in 1908 and 1913. The pictures on this page illustrate the famous 1908 standardization test at Brooklands, described in detail on page 12.

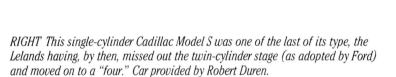

RIGHT This single-cylinder Cadillac Model S was one of the last of its type, the Lelands having, by then, missed out the twin-cylinder stage (as adopted by Ford) and moved on to a "four." Car provided by Robert Duren.

legendary Model T appeared. Everyone knows the rest of the story.)

Soon afterward, Leland used an invitation (to assist in the disposal of the Detroit Automobile Company's assets) to exploit *his* skill and experience. Leland & Faulconer had recently failed to sell Olds the idea of a much more powerful engine at no extra cost. The general manager at Olds had not been interested, so Leland showed the unit to Detroit Automobile's board. That engine was to prove the catalyst for a new marque. On the strength of its design, the Detroit Automobile Company was recapitalized to the tune of $300,000 – and renamed.

Cadillac is born

Antoine Laumet was the given name of the man who, in 1701, founded "the town on the strait" (*la ville d'étroit*): the "strait" was the water that separates today's Detroit in Michigan from Windsor, Ontario. History gives this leader among French settlers a more grandiose style: Le Sieur Antoine Laumet de la Mothe Cadillac.

In his book of personal comments and reminiscences, *Detroit Is My Own Home Town*, journalist Malcolm Bingay recorded how the local French Society had set plans in motion for a grand pageant to celebrate the second centenary of Laumet's arrival, thus reacquainting the populace with the name "Cadillac." That had been in 1901.

In August 1902 the Detroit Automobile Company became the Cadillac Automobile Company with Henry Leland as a director and technical consultant. The prototype Cadillac car, called the Model A, was completed in October. Its creation was overseen by Leland – now in his sixtieth year – and his son Wilfred. The leading light of the drawing board itself was Ernest Sweet. He was undoubtedly the Lelands' closest colleague at this stage. Sweet's chief associates were Alanson P. Brush and Frank Johnson.

Naturally enough, the first Cadillac borrowed directly from ideas which the Henrys, Ford and Leland, had shared – if only briefly – as well as from Olds with whom Leland was already trading. Naturally, too, Leland & Faulconer was to be the major supplier of mechanical components. This gave the Cadillac an integrity and a psychological advantage from the outset. The Cadillac's specification was, as it happened, less sophisticated than the materials and production techniques that gave the new marque an unprecedented assurance of quality. It was more expensive than the Oldsmobile; it would also cost more than the first production Ford (also a Model A) of 1903. On the other hand, Cadillac prices were to prove positively minute compared to those asked for early supercars, as epitomized by George N. Pierce's Great Arrow.

The Model A Cadillac had a single-cylinder 99 cu in (1.6-liter) under-floor engine, a two-speed planetary gearbox, and chain drive. A few cars were sold in late 1902; but it was the positive public reaction to the Cadillac at the New York Show in January 1903 that confirmed the sound thinking behind the Leland concept. In fact, Leland would not accept personal kudos for his undoubted genius, for he was a believer in teamwork and always gave credit where he felt it was due – usually in a general sense.

Like the Ford, the Cadillac took practical motoring beyond the "runabout" stage, and its reputation for reliability in difficult conditions spread worldwide. Soon it was being marketed abroad.

Early successes

In Britain, the Cadillac agent was Frederick S. Bennett, who already handled Oldsmobile. From 1903 he demonstrated the new car's capabilities in reliability events and hill climbs. Half a century later, in 1953, at the age of seventy-nine, Bennett set off on a successful re-run of the 1903 One Thousand Miles Trial in which he had won the prize for best performance with a car costing less than £200. He had kept the car and, reputedly, covered a quarter of a million miles in it during the intervening 50 years. In the early days, however, Bennett's greatest contribution to Cadillac lore was a spectacular demonstration even dearer to the perfectionist heart of Henry Leland.

By 1908 the Cadillac – basically unchanged, although sporting the by now fashionable hood – had reached the Model K development stage. Three examples of this type were taken straight from their crates (having been selected at random by Royal Automobile Club engineers) and driven from London to the newly opened Brooklands Motor Course in Surrey. Each car covered ten laps of the circuit for performance checks, and was then put into an individual garage behind the Members' hill, where each car was then dismantled. Into a fourth pristine garage were placed all the parts from the three cars, now completely stripped – nut from bolt, piston from rings – and all components were thoroughly jumbled up. The next move was for each car to be rebuilt in turn. At one stage the garages were flooded, and rust-speckled components littered the floor after the necessary pumping operations. Undeterred, the mechanics completed their task, and two of the cars started up immediately. Car number three had to wait a little longer, while the RAC specified and sent for 40 selected items from the spares department in London. Not only was each of the items in stock, but each fitted correctly and the car came together without difficulties. This classic "standardization" test was the public validation of Henry Leland's lifelong aim: to achieve and repeat near perfection in manufacture and, therefore, the absolute interchangeability of parts.

Sir Thomas (later Lord) Dewar of the famous whiskey-distilling family was a pioneer motorist. His interest in the automobile led him to provide for an award. Since 1906 it has been presented from time to time, at the discretion of the RAC's technical and engineering committee, for special achievements in the automotive field. For 1908 the RAC had no hesitation in presenting the Dewar Trophy to F. S. Bennett's Anglo-American Motor Car Company. Typically, Leland publicized the achievement as much inside the Cadillac works as out, saying that the honor of the award belonged to "every honest, sincere and conscientious" employee.

From 1904, Henry Leland was General Manager as well as a director of what, in 1905, became the Cadillac Motor Car Company. From this time, too, a new shaft-drive 4-cylinder car was developed. At first it was very expensive and sold in small numbers. A definitive version, the Thirty, was launched to replace all previous Cadillacs, including the single-cylinder range, of which close on 14,000 had been made by 1908.

CADILLAC Demi-Tonneau 1909			
ENGINE		**VEHICLE**	
Type	Vertical, in-line, water-cooled	Transmission	Three-speed manual gearbox
No. of cylinders	4	Driving wheels	Rear (via shaft)
Displacement	226 cu in (3700 cc)	Length	150 in (3800 mm)
Valve operation	Side	Wheelbase	106 in (2700 mm)
Carburation	One float-feed carburetor	Suspension	Rigid
BHP	30	Brakes	Rear only

NOTES
Cadillac 4-cylinder cars were made (with various sizes of engine) from 1905 to 1915, mostly from 1908. Early cars had three-speed planetary transmission, but a three-speed selective sliding gear was substituted in 1907.

The year 1908 was a momentous one. Not only was the world made aware of Henry Ford's "Tin Lizzie" or Model T, but also of a new type of company as it came into being: General Motors, founded by a Bostonian, William Crapo Durant. "No two men better understood the opportunity presented by the automobile in its early days," Alfred P. Sloan, President of GM for 14 years and its Chairman from 1937, once wrote of Durant and Ford. There was no one better qualified to make such a pronouncement.

Durant and GM

"Billy Durant never thought in dollars and cents, always in millions" – that was the bald view of journalist Malcolm Bingay.

Born in 1861, Durant was working for Joshua D. Dort, carriagemaker, in Flint, Michigan, as the automobile appeared on the horizon. Durant's belief in the new mode of transportation was so strong that he thought he

LEFT Henry Leland's grandson, Wilfred Jnr., demonstrates the magnitude of the Dewar Trophy – the prize that justified the Cadillac slogan: "Standard of the World."

BELOW AND OPPOSITE Cadillac moved into the modern era when it switched to four-cylinder engines. This 1909 model has a demi-tonneau body, and was provided for photography by Jerry Ray Nickel.

could take charge of the emerging industry. In 1904 he moved in on Buick, which was in financial trouble, and turned it around. Over 8000 Buicks had been built in 1908 when, on September 16, the General Motors Company was incorporated by Durant. He made Buick a member company on October 1. Oldsmobile came in on November 12. In 1909, Pontiac's forerunner Oakland (which owed much of its success to Alanson Brush, co-creator of the first Cadillac) joined the fold.

William Durant had had Cadillac on his shopping list for a long time, as his potential top-of-the-range marque: Durant's plan was to treat firms as satellites rather than to centralize. It was Wilfred, not Henry, Leland who negotiated for Cadillac, thus almost certainly saving General Motors from extinction.

Wilfred Leland had run the financial side of his father's businesses for many years, and it was only on terms dictated by him that Cadillac became part of General Motors in 1909. The price was $4.5 million and the condition was that the Lelands should retain control, which they did.

In 1910, the bankers called on Durant and his company chiefs to account for GM's rapidly deteriorating financial situation. They may have expected to liquidate. Wilfred Leland – the last man to be called, apparently – was able to show Cadillac in such a good light that the balance was tipped. Durant left, but General Motors was allowed a new lease of life. Buick remained the leading producer of the group, into which the Leland philosophy was being injected constantly. Walter P. Chrysler and Charles W. Nash, later to become famous car makers themselves, were among many early GM executives to be inspired by the wisdom of Henry Leland, whose own name would never grace an automobile. That was his way.

Electrical advances

Elderly but still energetic, Leland continued to lead. A most important Cadillac development is said to have been accelerated by a tragic incident of 1910 when Byron Carter, whose Cartercar company had been pulled into GM by Durant the previous year, died in hospital after being struck by a Cadillac's lashing starting handle. Leland was upset: he ordered his engineers to give priority to research into a self-starter. Frank Johnson was the key figure during this in-house development work.

Charles Franklin Kettering, soon to be a household name, was a brilliant Ohio University graduate who had been working on coil ignition; now Leland approached him to make a compact version of Johnson's self-starter. The outcome of the Leland-Kettering exchanges was that Cadillac became the first marque to offer the Delco (Dayton Engineering Laboratories) system of modern ignition: a landmark that was honored in Britain by the award of a second Dewar Trophy to Bennett's Anglo-American Motor Car Company.

The Lelands never introduced change for change's sake. However, such was the progress of the whole industry during these years that a new engine design was called for. The V8 configuration had been tried by other manufacturers, but only the long-established de Dion-Bouton company of France had actually put one into production. Wilfred Leland preferred the V8 to the straight-6, which was by now becoming popular in the United States, and his father accepted the idea after listening to his arguments concerning the use of lighter parts to permit higher engine revolutions. The first de Dion-Bouton V8 of 1910 had not been very efficient, and it was the updated version (introduced some two years later) that D. McCall White studied for Cadillac. White, a Scot, had worked for Daimler and Napier, two of Britain's outstanding early carmakers. Now he was applying his skills to creating the world's first volume-production V8 engine, which owed only its basic concept to de Dion and Bouton. The relative lightness, rigidity, and serviceability of this new unit were pure Cadillac. Besides, Leland's interchangeability laws were being pursued more strictly than ever, and Cadillac was still unrivaled for the accuracy of its machine tool settings. As a result, when it was ready for production in 1914, the new Cadillac offered a combination of specification and price which represented the best possible value (depending upon the style of bodywork ordered). In 1915, its first full year, 13,000 were built: an unprecedented quantity for a car in the over-$2000 class. The four-cylinder Cadillac was now phased out after a decade of consolidation, and would not be seen again for well over half a century, until the 1980s.

The era of the multicylinder Cadillac had arrived. Indeed, there has been a V8 type of engine in the Cadillac range ever since. That in itself makes this great marque unique.

ABOVE A youthful Charles Franklin Kettering and (LEFT) a less youthful but still sprightly Wilfred Leland.

RIGHT The definitive Cadillac four – a 1914 Model Thirty.

BELOW Typical American street scene during the heyday of the unreliable automobile – something that Henry Leland was determined to change.

THE LELAND LEGACY

Announcement of the V8 Cadillac had coincided with the outbreak of World War 1 in Europe. The United States of America was not involved industrially straight away, though, and during the war years, Cadillac's production increased to 18,000 and then 20,000 cars annually – and consisted solely of V8s.

In its use of side valves (when Buick had overhead valves), and in its somewhat outdated form of semielliptic rear springing, the Cadillac showed itself not to be *avant-garde* throughout. On the other hand, the 90-degree V8 engine of more than 300 cu in (5 liters) provided a superb road performance for those days. As the country became more involved in Europe's affairs, so the US War Department tested and selected suitable products. Potential staff cars underwent a 2000-mile test, and those shortlisted continued on a further 5000-mile "final." Following the results of these events, the Cadillac became standard issue for military brass hats, General John J. Pershing included.

Enter Mr. Sloan – GM's savior

Although its founder, William Durant, had been ousted as head of General Motors following the bankers' intervention of 1910, he had continued to be hyperactive from a business point of view. In the early part of 1916 he contacted numerous suppliers to the automobile industry, including Alfred P. Sloan Jr.

Alfred Sloan (1875-1966), chief executive of General Motors for nearly a quarter of a century, was the grandson of a Methodist minister and schoolmaster. Born in New Haven, Connecticut, he was brought up in Brooklyn, New York, from the age of ten. His first job after graduation was as general factotum for the Hyatt Roller Bearing Company of New Jersey. He was twenty years old and took home $50 a month. Three years later he brought Hyatt back from the red into the black. Thereafter it did not take him long to become Hyatt's general manager (at twenty-four!). Henry Leland was 14 years his senior, and Sloan "looked upon him as an elder not only in age but in engineering wisdom."

Sloan learned from Leland "the need for greater accuracy in our products to meet the exacting standards of interchangeable parts." It was Sloan's own declaration that Cadillac engineering had had an important influence on his Hyatt operations and upon the industry at large.

At the age of forty, Sloan was requested to meet "soft-spoken and ingratiating" William Durant. Durant wanted to buy Hyatt, and his bid was successful. With this and several other firms – including Delco –

Durant formed United Motors with Sloan as chief executive, selling components to a number of manufacturers and assemblers – including General Motors.

An earlier purchase by Durant had been that of the Chevrolet Motor Company; and in 1917, through acquisition of shares, he was able to clamber aboard General Motors once again. It was soon after this that the Lelands resigned, following a fundamental disagreement with Durant over their proposed use of a new Cadillac factory for Liberty aero engine manufacture.

The founding of Lincoln

Such was the Leland reputation that the brilliant father-and-son team had little difficulty, as independents, in obtaining initial finance. Between August 1917 and January 1919, their new company built 6500 aero engines for the American war effort. Once more, the idea of a "Leland Industries" was eschewed: their new company was, instead, named after the president whom Henry Leland had admired so much in his youth – Abraham Lincoln.

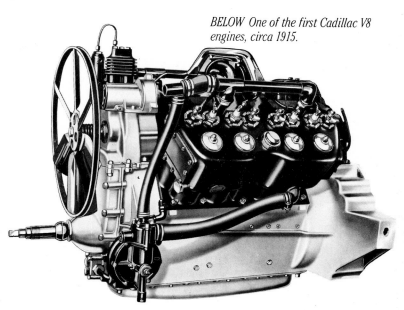

BELOW One of the first Cadillac V8 engines, circa 1915.

ABOVE Series 314A Fisher-bodied Tourer, dating from 1927 and provided by Lawrence Seidell.

LEFT 1922 Type 61 V8 Limousine – a direct descendant of the original eight-cylinder Cadillac, provided by Don Reel.

RIGHT Alfred P. Sloan, the man who built GM, pictured in later life by Karsh of Ottawa.

PREVIOUS PAGES Early LaSalle Series 303 of 1927, provided by Leonard Piskiewicz. (Note the "pilot ray" lamp.)

Ernest Sweet and Frank Johnson were among those who moved with the Lelands, and the first Lincoln car, with a 60-degree side-valve V8 engine of 350 cu in (5.8 liters), was announced as early as September 1920. If Henry Leland had a weakness, however, it was a certain lack of adventure in matters of style. By the time he sought the help of the top bodywork specialists, the postwar recession had set in.

The Lelands had done well to get their new enterprise off the ground but they needed further sponsorship. In the past it had been forthcoming; but now some bad luck prevented it. The Lincoln company was sent a vastly excessive tax bill by the US Government. The clerical error was corrected subsequently but, at the time, it was enough to force the Lincoln Motor Company into receivership, and thence into Ford ownership early in 1922. Henry Ford did not give the Lelands the freedom of action to which they were accustomed, and after only a few months father and son left and went their own way once more.

Henry Leland was now in his eightieth year. He lived on for the best part of a decade, doodling with design (including rear engines and four-wheel-drive systems) and remaining active in community affairs. Wilfred Leland turned his engineering and business talents to the mining industry. Their old colleague Frank Johnson would, in due course, play a big part in Lincoln's development as another great marque.

Without Henry Leland there would have been no Lincoln and no Cadillac, and the development of the automobile industry would have been much impoverished.

Durant's second coming – and going

William Durant did not take proper advantage of his return to power. It is true that he was responsible for General Motors' great expansion in the 1918 to 1920 period. Not only did he bring in Chevrolet as a marque to challenge Ford, but he was responsible for GM acquiring a major holding in Fisher, the auto body company in which Leland's "interchangeability" theories had been applied for some years. McLaughlin of Oshawa, Ontario, became General Motors of Canada Ltd; component supply groups to be brought in naturally included United Motors, of which Alfred Sloan was president. Sloan was to become the guiding force at General Motors within a very short time.

Cadillac had been an efficient company under the Lelands, giving GM's bankers little cause for concern. Such was not the case with other satellites of the corporation, and Durant's return spelled imminent financial crisis. The national slump of 1920 exposed the dangers inherent in Durant's organization. At the end of November 1920 he resigned his GM presidency. Durant remained an optimistic speculator, although in his subsequent business dealings he would never hit the dizzy heights that he had attained on two occasions in the forming of General Motors. Alfred Sloan described him as brilliant, daring and reckless – "a great man, with a great weakness: he could create but not administer." William Durant, who lived to old age through many smaller-scale crises, does not figure in this story again.

For the time being, Pierre Du Pont became President and chief steadying influence at GM. In 1923 that task went to Alfred Sloan.

LASALLE
Sports Phaeton
1927

ENGINE

Type	90° V, in-line, water-cooled
No. of cylinders	8
Bore/stroke	3.15 × 4.9 in (80 × 125 mm)
Displacement	303 cu in (4967 cc)
Valve operation	Side
Compression ratio	5.0:1
Carburation	One updraft carburetor
BHP	75 gross

VEHICLE

Transmission	Three-speed manual gearbox
Driving wheels	Rear
Length	197 in (5000 mm)
Wheelbase	125 in (3175 mm)
Weight (approx.)	4200 lb (1900 kg)
Steering	Worm & sector
Suspension	Rigid, semi-elliptics
Brakes	Drum (four-wheel)

NOTES

First year of LaSalle marque. Also first use of 'second-generation' Cadillac V8 engine. Style by Earl; execution by Fisher.

In his Hyatt Roller Bearing days, Sloan had used a Conrad (it "was a lemon") and a Pittsburgh-built Autocar (it "worked better") for his early travels. By 1910, however, he had reached a position of free choice – and he chose a Cadillac.

Alfred Sloan's continued success lay in his appreciation of the needs of the manufacturer as well as the whims of the customer. Management and organization were at his fingertips; yet in the consolidation of GM he never overlooked the need for individuality in the product as well as technical and economical progress. Numerous GM-owned car companies disappeared quickly in the early 1920s, but five were to become solid GM divisions: Chevrolet and Oakland (Pontiac) at the bargain end of the market, Buick and Oldsmobile in the middle ground. Cadillac, Sloan promised, would stay as the flagship marque – and so it did. Sloan never forgot the impression Henry Leland had made upon him, nor the excellence of his own first Cadillac.

That Cadillac had been bought as a chassis with Sloan's choice of made-to-measure bodywork, presumably by the Fisher company. The father of the Fisher brothers (Alfred, Charles, Edward, Fred, Lawrence and William) had been their teacher at his small carriage and wagon shop in Norwalk, Ohio. In 1908 their Fisher Body Company had been set up, and in 1910 they had received their first block order for 150 Cadillac bodies.

All the brothers were regarded as "skilled artisans" by Sloan, who came to know them all. Lawrence Fisher was to play the biggest part in the post-Leland progress of Cadillac, where he became General Manager in 1925. Sloan (who admitted having fitted small wheels to his first Cadillac back in 1910) and Fisher worked well together. They shared the view that, when it came to making a sale, one of an automobile's greatest assets was its appearance.

Style and image

Styling had not figured in Leland's priority list for the Cadillac. All that was about to change as a result of Lawrence Fisher's first nationwide dealer tour as General Manager.

Hollywood stars were already beginning to express themselves, or at least create an image, by the cars they drove. One man to recognize the possibilities was Don Lee who sold Cadillacs in Los Angeles, where he owned a body works: not the traditional kind, but what might be called a customizing shop. Lawrence Fisher was shown the facility, which offered the lowering and lengthening of chassis frames as well as

22

exciting bodywork; he also met the chief designer, Harley J. Earl, whose father's body shops had been bought by Lee.

The acquisition of young Earl had been a stroke of luck for Don Lee: but he would not be keeping him for very long. Harley Earl signed a contract with Lawrence Fisher and, early in 1926, he moved from California to Michigan and became a full-time styling consultant to Cadillac. This was a completely new role in the automobile industry, yet fully supported by Sloan, who saw it as a way of overcoming the "badge engineering" problem which arises when corporate decisions are taken on behalf of revered names. Indeed, it led to the creation of a new marque name almost immediately.

The creation of LaSalle

For 1927, Fisher and Sloan agreed that it was time to produce a gap filler: that gap being the considerable financial one that lay between the most expensive Buick and the cheapest Cadillac. (General Motors was, by this time, endeavoring to offer a variety of cars across the complete price spectrum.) Following the precedent set by Henry Leland, GM chose to name its new product after another French explorer of lofty title: Robert Cavelier, Sieur de La Salle, the man who had claimed the Mississippi region of North America for France in 1682, only to be murdered by his few surviving men in a bungled expedition five years later. "His" car was to lead a short life, too, but a distinguished one just the same.

The LaSalle was announced in March 1927 and proved itself an immediate hit, being a compact companion to the Cadillac which, in its least expensive form, sold for around $3000. Buick's costliest offering was priced at $2000. The basic LaSalle had a neat $2500 price tag, plus the prestige implied by Cadillac quality. As for performance, one lightly "hotted up" example sped around GM's own test track at an average speed of over 95 mph (153 km/h) for ten hours. The test would have been carried on for longer but for a broken oil pipe.

Such high speed was accounted for by the use of a new version of the 90-degree V8 Cadillac power unit, displacing 303 cu in (4967 cc) – hence the new model's "303" designation.

Since the Lelands' departure in 1917, there had been no letup in the work of maintaining their standards. In 1923, Ernest Seaholm had succeeded Benjamin Anibal as Cadillac's senior engineer. He was very conscious of a certain vibration period in the existing V8 engines. The availability of Charles Franklin Kettering's fertile mind was put to advantage here, and the 1924 Cadillac range had featured his two-plane crankshaft which gave an already-fine power unit complete smoothness of running at all speeds. (In 1924, too, Cadillac became an early user of four-wheel braking.)

The 1927 LaSalle's engine was further developed by another of Lawrence Fisher's new recruits, called Owen Milton Nacker. His purpose was, primarily, to produce a new and dramatic range of Cadillac engines, as described in Chapter Three.

LEFT AND ABOVE LEFT 1929 was the last of the industry's successful pioneering years, and it saw the creation of such fine cars as this close-coupled Cadillac Series 341 Sedan. In the fall came the Wall Street crash. This car provided for photography by Sam Kaplan.

PREVIOUS PAGES First Series 303 LaSalle Sports Phaeton, dating from 1927, provided by Garth Carrier.

23

Corporate styling

Harley Earl's LaSalle, smoothly curved and enticingly colored, was probably the first example of a car created as an artistic entity. Earl had used such new aids as clay models when working for Don Lee; now his special talents would be put to work for the whole corporation. Having made sure that the next Cadillac range would be thoroughly up-to-date, Alfred Sloan established an Art and Color Section (later called the Styling Section) which would provide services to the other car divisions – after some initial reluctance on their part. The first to benefit would be Chevrolet, locked in combat with Ford whose one-model policy was being transformed by the replacement of the Model T with the completely new and modern Model A.

Before establishing himself in his new role, Earl accompanied Fisher on a tour of Europe, generally recognized to be the seat of artistic and technical creativity; although it was not, of course, as advanced in production technology, in which America led the world. In fact, the first LaSalle had borne a number of European features, most of which seemed to relate to the Hispano-Suiza which was, after all, one of the world's fastest and most expensive road cars.

The American market had reached one of its most buoyant periods, and Cadillac-LaSalle output exceeded 50,000 units for the first time in the 1928 model year. There would not be a better year for the salesmen for a long time to come.

The 1929 season began well. Firsts for the Cadillac and LaSalle

LEFT Harley Earl – the man who brought style to Cadillac and LaSalle, shown here in a pose that suggests the flamboyance of his later years at GM. Hispano-Suiza was the marque he chose as inspiration for the first LaSalle's styling.

RIGHT This 1928 close-coupled Cadillac Series 341 Sedan was provided by Robert Duren.

BELOW A 1929 Cadillac Series 341B Convertible with dual side-mounted spare wheels. Car provided by Don Reel.

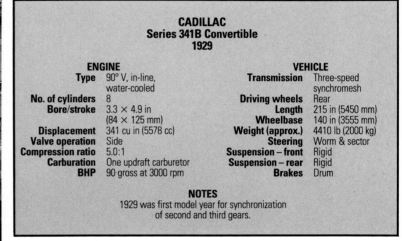

CADILLAC
Series 341B Convertible
1929

ENGINE		VEHICLE	
Type	90° V, in-line, water-cooled	**Transmission**	Three-speed synchromesh
No. of cylinders	8	**Driving wheels**	Rear
Bore/stroke	3.3 × 4.9 in (84 × 125 mm)	**Length**	215 in (5450 mm)
Displacement	341 cu in (5578 cc)	**Wheelbase**	140 in (3555 mm)
Valve operation	Side	**Weight (approx.)**	4410 lb (2000 kg)
Compression ratio	5.0:1	**Steering**	Worm & sector
Carburation	One updraft carburetor	**Suspension – front**	Rigid
BHP	90 gross at 3000 rpm	**Suspension – rear**	Rigid
		Brakes	Drum

NOTES
1929 was first model year for synchronization
of second and third gears.

marques were chromium plating, safety glass, and synchromesh. The last feature, which operated on second and third gears, had been patented as early as 1922 by Earl Thompson, who subsequently became Cadillac's transmission development engineer. Cadillac shared synchromesh with LaSalle initially, before passing it on to GM juniors Buick, Oldsmobile, Pontiac and Chevrolet.

Sloan's way ahead

General Motors could, at this stage, look back at more than five years of continuous expansion (since the brief slump of the early 1920s) under the dynamic leadership of Alfred Sloan. In those years he had stage-managed further additions to the corporation's interests abroad (notably Holden of Australia, Vauxhall of England and Opel of Germany) and streamlined the organization at home. He had ensured that GM had all the resources it needed to become the biggest, and in many ways the best, company of its kind, while retaining a strong element of decentralization for its divisions. Many other companies came to adopt the General Motors way of management – Sloan's way.

Part of the plan had been to keep Cadillac at the top, and that had succeeded, too. Cadillac's chief rivals were: Packard, who had made a V12 (the Twin Six) for a few years but was now back to in-line engines; the Lincoln, which still had the Leland stamp about it, and was popular with presidents; Chrysler, soon to produce a rival, but this company was still young. The Duesenberg and the Pierce-Arrow, the Stutz and the Springfield Rolls-Royce were magnificent, exclusive, vulnerable and doomed. For the moment, however, there were enough folk prepared to pay the price.

Cadillac itself was on the eve of producing its new, secret defense package – to secure its special position.

The failure of the New York Stock Exchange in October 1929 was to lead to a period of depression that would cripple and destroy in every area of human endeavor.

OVERCOMING THE DEPRESSION

To many people, the first years of the Depression represent the period of ultimate development in American luxury car design from both the engineer's and the artist's standpoints. Engineering and art were given equal billing in the land that created the annual model change: this was especially true in the vast, image-sensitive halls of the General Motors Corporation.

By this time, GM could afford to invest in the prestige of Cadillac, to ensure its sales superiority over potential rivals. So it was that, only a few weeks after the Wall Street Crash (and in another part of Manhattan), Lawrence Fisher launched the most sophisticated Cadillac of them all: the 452 chassis. It was not in the Duesenberg category for sheer performance, but this new luxury machine was nevertheless the talk of New York's automobile show in January 1930: Cadillac was about to make history by becoming the only marque ever to market a 16-cylinder car in anything like regular production quantities.

Nor was this just a gimmick of doubtful value for, alongside his V16, Owen Nacker had developed a V12 too! But it was the surprise announcement of the sixteen that put Cadillac firmly on its pedestal as America's supercar leader for the 1930s. Although prelaunch rumors had tended to cluster around the V12, the smaller engine's announcement was in fact held back for several months so that the company would be able to spread the exciting news over a longer period.

Cadillac's first V16 was a thing of great beauty. Its cylinder banks were disposed at an angle of 45 degrees and topped with attractively ribbed valve covers. Visually, the engine was enhanced by the careful positioning of electrical components and other essential attachments, so that the view upon opening the elegant hood was as uncluttered as it was satisfying.

The overhead valves and rockers were pushrod operated from a central camshaft and, with a compression ratio of 5.5 to 1, the claimed power was 175 hp at 3400 rpm. Over the whole project hovered not only Charles Kettering but Henry Leland, whose precepts of accuracy and material quality continued to bring credit to the rapidly expanding automobile industry of America, and to the name of Cadillac in particular. Two Cadillac updraft carburetors were employed initially, and the performance was outstanding for the period (if not for the specification). With a sporting body and "high" rear-axle ratio, 100 mph (160 km/h) was possible; but usually the weight of the body would dictate a "lower" ratio, and in such cases 90 mph (145 km/h) would be a more accurate maximum speed claim.

What every version of the 452 Cadillac possessed was an unprecedented refinement which was the envy of potential rivals. The type name came from the 452 cu in (7.4 liters) which the 16 pistons displaced. Miles covered per gallon of fuel consumed reached double figures only on cruising journeys.

PREVIOUS PAGES William Jahant's 452C Convertible Victoria was built for Robert Montgomery. The four-bar bumper design identifies it as a 1933 car.

CADILLAC	
Series 452 Phaeton	
1930	
ENGINE	
Type	45° V, in-line, water-cooled
No. of cylinders	16
Bore/stroke	3 × 4 in (76 × 102 mm)
Displacement	452 cu in (7406 cc)
Valve operation	Overhead
Compression ratio	5.5:1
Carburation	Two updraft carburetors
BHP	175 gross at 3400 rpm
VEHICLE	
Transmission	Three-speed synchromesh
Driving wheels	Rear
Length	220 in (5600 mm)
Wheelbase	148 in (3760 mm)
Weight (approx.)	4630 lb (2100 kg)
Steering	Worm & sector
Suspension – front	Rigid, semi-elliptics
Suspension – rear	Rigid, semi-elliptics
Brakes	Drum, mechanical

NOTES
Cadillac's were the only 16-cylinder automotive engines to be produced for any length of time (1930 to 1940).

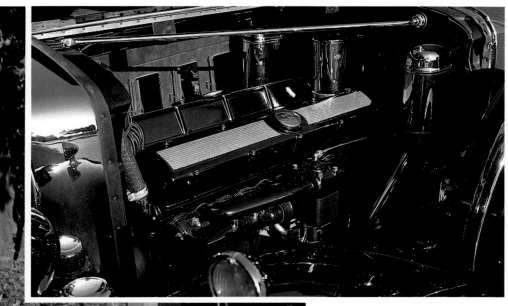

ABOVE AND LEFT The 1930 Series 452 Cadillac, with its magnificent narrow-angle V16 power unit, could touch 100 mph (160 km/h) in some forms – though probably not quite when fitted with this All-Weather Phaeton bodywork. Car provided by Paul Shinnerer.

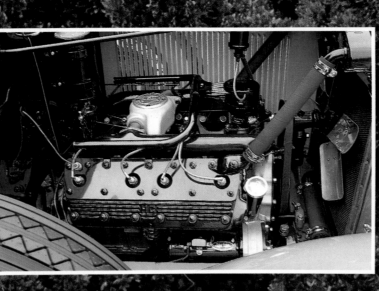

Fashionable extras on this Fisher-bodied 1930 Series 340 LaSalle Convertible Coupe (provided by Lawrence Klein) included "pilot ray" light. A V8 engine (INSET) and Earl's styling put LaSalle firmly in the Cadillac mold.

It took some time for the full enormity of the Depression to be realized and for its lasting effects to be felt; the 1933 model year proved to be the worst for most surviving manufacturers. Cadillac had taken full advantage of the brief sales boom created by the 452 series. In 1930 and 1931, over 3000 were sold; but during the four years from 1932 to 1935 only a further 500 appeared: just 50 of these were produced in the latter year.

The 452 was joined by the 370 series in September 1930. This V12 had all the same qualities as the V16 on an only slightly reduced scale. It shared the 4-in (102 mm) stroke of its bigger brother, but was bored out from 3 in (76 mm) to 3.12 in (79 mm), giving a capacity of 370 cu in or about 6 liters. Nearly 10,000 of these 135 hp cars were produced over the same six seasons at a similarly dwindling rate.

The Cadillacs of this period were given suffix letters to identify the model year: for twelves and sixteens, A represents 1931, B is for 1932, C for 1933 and D for 1934-35; 1930 cars do not have a suffix. The range was of course buoyed up by the V8 Cadillac and LaSalle range, but the production figures did not look good on paper: from a record high of well over 40,000 cars in 1928, the combined marques were down to around the 6000 mark in 1933, their worst year of all.

Bodies beautiful

Besides technical excellence, and the umbrella of GM, it was style that enabled Cadillac to survive these lean years. The creator of LaSalle, Harley Earl, made his presence felt in every GM range, but most notably

ABOVE European body specialists made their mark on Cadillac occasionally. The Dresden company formed by Heinrich Gläser in the 19th century made this one-off body on the 1931 Cadillac Series 355A chassis. Car provided by Gaines Adcock.

RIGHT Delicate window frames and a sloping windshield are the key features of this elegant Fleetwood-bodied Cadillac "Madame X" Series 452A Sedan on the 1931 V16 chassis, provided by Owen Crain. The mysterious name was a characteristically theatrical allusion from Harley Earl.

in the Cadillac. Moreover, the body maker's expertise was to a considerable degree available within the GM family. Among the most respected practitioners in America was the long-established Fleetwood company, based in the Pennsylvania town of that name. The Fisher Body company was already closely linked with Cadillac and other Detroit car makers when it had taken over Fleetwood. A year later (in 1926) Fisher and Fleetwood had become a fully integrated division of GM.

From the winter of 1930-31, when its craftsmen had moved to Detroit, the Fleetwood name was to become even more tightly tied to Cadillac. If "Body by Fisher" added prestige to the corporation's products, "Fleetwood" possessed an even more impressive cachet (and it is liberally sprinkled over today's model range titles). Despite the hard times, a wide variety of offerings kept Cadillac ahead in what was left of the market during the Depression when, even though neither Cadillac nor LaSalle could always run at a profit, GM as a whole did manage to stay in the

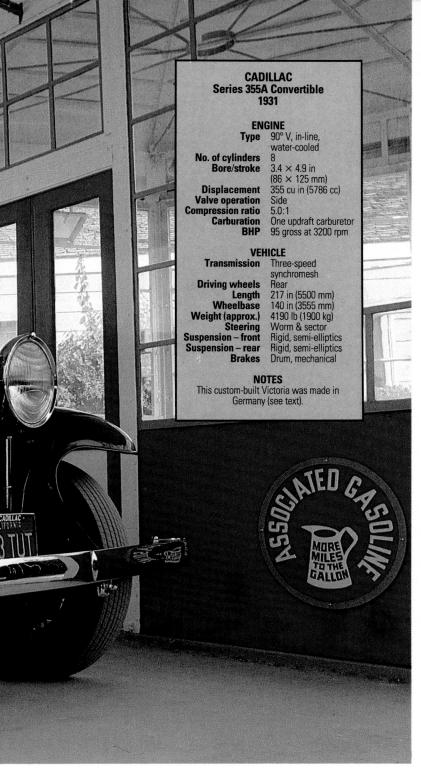

**CADILLAC
Series 355A Convertible
1931**

ENGINE

Type	90° V, in-line, water-cooled
No. of cylinders	8
Bore/stroke	3.4 × 4.9 in (86 × 125 mm)
Displacement	355 cu in (5786 cc)
Valve operation	Side
Compression ratio	5.0:1
Carburation	One updraft carburetor
BHP	95 gross at 3200 rpm

VEHICLE

Transmission	Three-speed synchromesh
Driving wheels	Rear
Length	217 in (5500 mm)
Wheelbase	140 in (3555 mm)
Weight (approx.)	4190 lb (1900 kg)
Steering	Worm & sector
Suspension – front	Rigid, semi-elliptics
Suspension – rear	Rigid, semi-elliptics
Brakes	Drum, mechanical

NOTES

This custom-built Victoria was made in Germany (see text).

black throughout, thanks to Sloan's system. In the good times, the gigantic spider's web of GM might not create a particularly attractive image; in those depressed days of the early 1930s, however, its broad and solid business base was the envy of many. It is worth looking at the quality opposition at this juncture.

Peers and rivals

The Duesenberg, a stunning performer by all standards, was running out of time despite owner Errett Lobban Cord's not-unjustified claim that it was the "world's finest" car. Cord's empire (which included the Auburn and, of course, the Cord) was wound up in 1937, and by this time America's other great sports car, the European-style Stutz, had also gone.

Reo (the marque created by Ransom Eli Olds when he had forsaken his original company in 1904) had been a steady producer of middle-class machines in the 1920s. As with so many other companies, Reo made its lunge at the prestige market just as the slump took hold. Its elegant 1933 Flying Cloud Custom Royale had Duesenberg overtones but, good as it was, it had negligible trade backup. Olds resigned after a 1933 boardroom row and cooperation with Franklin could save neither marque.

Former GM chief Charles W. Nash was now a successful producer in his own right. He payed only lip service to the luxury market, whereas his old colleague Walter P. Chrysler – by now running America's number three automobile corporation – produced, in the Custom Imperial straight-8, one of the last classic chassis to make the most of the artistic and technical capabilities of the great body houses such as Derham, Le Baron and Murphy.

Ford was bringing the V8 to the popular motoring world but made use of the Lincoln name to announce a V12 for 1932: two years behind Cadillac. Ford, like Chrysler, was big enough to weather the storm. Pierce-Arrow went bankrupt, however, and helped Studebaker do likewise – although the latter did revive later.

Unquenchable optimism characterized many small companies. There was one potential Cadillac rival among them that stood head and shoulders above the rest – only to be cut down in its prime. The Indianapolis-built Marmon had established a fine pedigree of advanced engineering when the Depression struck. Undeterred, Marmon proceeded with a magnificent 200 hp 490 cu in (8.1-liter) V16 range of dream cars. Extensive use of alloys kept the weight down, and each car was guaranteed to have averaged 100 mph (160 km/h) for two laps of its famous local "brickyard" before delivery. At $5000 to $6000, the price was comparable to that of the only other serious V16. However, it came a year after the Cadillac, and Marmon could not handle this disadvantage, coupled with the rapid drop in demand during those worst years, 1931 to 1933. Howard Marmon sank his personal fortune into a final recovery effort but all to no avail.

There remained one other Cadillac rival in what might be called the Depression's white elephant marketplace, one that cannot be left out of this account: Packard. Like Rolls-Royce, this marque had come into

being through one man saying to another: "We could make a better car ourselves." (In this case the Packard brothers, James W. and William D., had been discussing their 1898 Winton.) In 1915, Packard had followed closely on Cadillac's heels in multiple cylinder exploration; Cadillac's original V8 had been announced for only a short time when Packard came out with a V12. A switch to straight-8 had been made in the early 1920s, but, for the early 1930s, a new V12 put Packard firmly back into the top bracket of acceptable exotica. The distinctive prow, the characteristic red hubs, and the restrained, balanced, unadorned lines provided by Ray Dietrich and other styling greats ensured that Packard kept Cadillac's marketing men on their toes. Packard was also well enough established to move quickly into the popular car field, which helped it turn a $7 million loss in 1932 to a measurable profit in the following financial year.

Cadillac, therefore, could never afford to rest on its laurels, and Lawrence Fisher made it his job to keep the marque just as up-to-date technically as it was aesthetically.

Independent front suspension introduced

Ride and handling are accepted partners in modern terminology, but neither word would have meant much in the 1920s. If a car could be under full control and its passengers remain reasonably comfortable, then the springing medium was doing its stuff. Quite apart from his outstanding business skills, GM chief Alfred Sloan was also something of a connoisseur of automobile development, and his trips abroad tended to show him just how far European suspension design was ahead in this field. It was at Sloan's invitation that André Dubonnet visited Detroit, with the result that GM bought patent rights to the Frenchman's design of independent suspension, known as the "knee action" type.

LEFT Brilliant styling characterized the mighty V16 Cadillacs, of which this fastback for the 1933 Chicago World's Fair was one of the most celebrated examples.

BELOW Cars and stars went together in the 1930s: this convertible Victoria was custom-built by Fleetwood on a 1933 Series 452C (V16) chassis for actor Robert Montgomery. Provided by William Jahant.

ABOVE: In the Post-Depression period, the V8-engined models saved the day for Cadillac. This 1933 Fisher-bodied Series 355C was provided for photography by Leonard Urlik.

One of Lawrence Fisher's senior engineers was Maurice Olley, who had been a confidant of Henry Royce in designing the World War 1 Rolls-Royce Eagle V12 aero engine. There was a strong affinity between the aims of the Rolls-Royce and Cadillac organizations. Maurice Olley had moved to America as soon as Rolls-Royce had begun doing business there and had become chief engineer at the Springfield, Massachusetts, works. (It is noteworthy that Rolls-Royce had chosen to base itself in Springfield rather than Detroit – in order to be different, yes, but also because of the wealth of skill and experience to be found in the New England factories, where Henry Leland had learned the secrets of repetitive precision machining so many years earlier.) As chief engineer at Springfield, Olley had been able to help Rolls-Royce achieve good ride characteristics – something in which, for no good reason, Britain appeared to lag behind.

Olley had done much to improve the Rolls-Royce image in the United States when, in November 1930, he accepted Lawrence Fisher's invitation to join Cadillac, and put his highly practicable theories at the disposal of his new employers. With help from Henry M. Crane, Olley developed a simple rig which provided the subjective, but invaluable, evidence that was needed for a positive decision on the general use of independent front suspension, which Cadillac adopted in 1934. This featured unequal-length wishbones and coil springs for the first time in a luxury car, and meant that Cadillac was again one up on Packard. It also meant that the power unit could be moved forward and all passengers accommodated within the wheelbase, thus changing the balance and style of the automobile completely.

It was in 1934 that Nicholas Dreystadt became general manager of Cadillac, and he led it to its next peak of success three years later. Cadillac would never again have to find a way across a trough as deep as that of 1932-33. Another new man, whose clear thinking and light touch were to have a big effect on Cadillac's future, joined General Motors in that great turnaround year of 1934.

Attention to style maintained

Aged twenty-two, he had caught the eye of Harley Earl through his work as artist in an advertising agency – or maybe it was some of his action sketches of early sports car racing on the Collier family estate near Tarrytown, New York. He had even designed a badge for those young bloods who invented the Automobile Racing Club of America (it would

lead to the Sports Car Club of America). The son of a Pennsylvania Buick dealer, his name was William Mitchell: a name that would become almost as legendary as that of Harley Earl.

Earl had produced some stunning styles for the Cadillacs of the early 1930s: as we have seen, his Art and Color Section was renamed the Styling Section. His intentions were always clear: "My primary purpose has been to lengthen and lower the American automobile – at times in reality; in appearance, always." "Oblongs are more attractive than squares," added Earl on that occasion, by way of explanation.

The big advantage (and maybe disadvantage) for Earl was his economic proximity to the body maker. Back in 1929 he had been aghast when Buick production engineers "rearranged" the proportions he had proposed for that year's model, dubbed the "pregnant Buick." Earl's Cadillacs suffered no such interference. The year 1932 was the last for the "Hispano-Suiza" shape, which Earl exploited to the full in his rakish "Madame X," named after a character in a play. For 1932 there was an increasing roundness; the wing lines looked just a little unsure of themselves, and the skirted effect (pioneered by Reo in the previous season) tended to exaggerate the combination of convex and concave curves. Also in 1933, Cadillac and other GM cars were the first to feature NDVs – Fisher's swiveling "No-Draft Ventilators" – in the front windows.

The top models in 1934 were the definitive and magnificent D series of V16s, V12s and, of course, bread-and-butter V8s. Earl increased windshield widths by some 4 in (100 mm), and he introduced the so-called pontoon wing shape which gave the cars a heavier look – but a thoroughly integrated one, for the outline remained convex throughout. This established a basic configuration for the "Great American Fender" which would continue until Earl produced his famous fins 14 years later. Key cars of 1934 were the 452D Victoria convertible, on a 12 ft 10 in (3.9 m) wheelbase, and fastback two-door sedan by Fleetwood. Both were beautifully proportioned, and the latter was previewed at the 1933 World's Fair in Chicago where it was the undisputed star. While the side-mounted spare wheel was shown to be a fading fashion, whitewall tires had come to stay by now; the general impression was one of just the right amount of decoration.

LaSalle individuality

From its earliest days, in 1927, Cadillac's companion LaSalle had fulfilled its role: to extend Cadillac's perceived quality into a lower price bracket. There had been a subtle change, however, and this had turned LaSalle more and more into a badge-engineered Cadillac. One line of argument was that it made little sense to have two marques when either – maybe both – could be dropped with economic justification. For 1931, 1932 and 1933 they shared the very same specification of side-valve V8 engine; they looked similar, too.

Another line of argument was that LaSalle's individuality should be reestablished, and who better to present that argument than Harley Earl himself? He had created the marque. Now he would recreate it – if he won his argument, which he did.

The 1934 LaSalle was certainly distinctive, with a slender radiator cowl and the first example of a single-pressing steel cabin section, Fisher's "turret top": an important advance in body manufacture. The car also had independent front suspension and hydraulic brakes. To keep costs down, an Oldsmobile straight-8 engine was used. The new LaSalle was a good-looker, but its row of five portholes along each side of the hood gave a warning of GM gewgaws to come. Once again, LaSalle lived; Cadillac, meantime, kept its "V-engines only" reputation.

Chrysler was in trouble selling its brave but ill-conceived Airflow. On the other hand, Packard's One Twenty model offered traditional style at a low price from 1935; and there were other new rivals. The trouble was that LaSalle could no longer boast a Cadillac power unit in its advertising. Alfred Sloan used to say that General Motors made a profit during Depression because of its ability to react to circumstances quickly. For example, whenever there was a drop in demand, internal cost controls were applied at the earliest opportunity. Perhaps on this occasion the decision to change LaSalle's engine configuration had been an overreaction? Well, GM's policymaking groups were not too proud to reverse a decision in the interests of the company and so, after three seasons of unintentional kinship with Oldsmobile, LaSalle was made to revert to its

CADILLAC
Series 370D Town Car
1935

ENGINE

Type	45° V, in-line, water-cooled
No. of cylinders	12
Bore/stroke	3.15 × 4 in (80 × 102 mm)
Displacement	370 cu in (6030 cc)
Valve operation	Overhead
Compression ratio	5.5:1
Carburation	Two updraft carburetors
BHP	135 gross at 3400 rpm

VEHICLE

Transmission	Three-speed synchromesh
Driving wheels	Rear
Length	220 in (5600 mm)
Wheelbase	143 in (3630 mm)
Weight (approx.)	4410 lb (2000 kg)
Steering	Worm & sector
Suspension	Rigid, semi-elliptics
Brakes	Drum, mechanical

NOTES

Brakes were vacuum-servo-assisted. (Cadillac was about to start a switch to hydraulic operation.) Seven-passenger bodywork by Fleetwood.

1937 was the last year for the V12 Cadillac engine, as fitted to this Series 85 Formal Sedan (provided by Ted Davidson). However, a new multicylinder power unit, the side-valve wide-angle V16, would be introduced for 1938.

original allotted role as the first cousin of the Cadillac V8.

On the whole, automotive history has proved the "companion" marque to be a failure. The customer, enthusiast or not, prefers a familiar name. General Motors had proved this earlier, when each marque, apart from Chevrolet, had been given a companion. Buick had the Marquette, Oakland the Pontiac, and Oldsmobile the Viking. (The Pontiac was the exception; it survived and the Oakland vanished.) Cadillac's companion was to conform to pattern in due course, even though it was respected and (apparently) well established. For the moment, however, it had a new lease of life. In 1937, the industry's best year of the decade, LaSalle made a record number of cars – over 30,000 of them – cashing in on its new 125 hp 340 cu in (5.3-liter) V8 engine which, although still a side-valve, gave LaSalle its best-ever performance.

CADILLAC
Series 60 Special Sedan
1941

ENGINE

Type	90° V, in-line, water-cooled
No. of cylinders	8
Bore/stroke	3.5 × 4.5 in (89 × 114 mm)
Displacement	346 cu in (5676 cc)
Valve operation	Side
Compression ratio	7.0:1
Carburation	One downdraft carburetor
BHP	150 gross at 3400 rpm

VEHICLE

Transmission	Three-speed manual synchromesh
Driving wheels	Rear
Length	213 in (5400 mm)
Wheelbase	126 in (3200 mm)
Weight (approx.)	4210 lb (1910 kg)
Final drive	Hypoid bevel
Suspension – front	Independent
Suspension – rear	Rigid
Brakes	Drum

NOTES
1941 was the fourth and final season for this composite-bodied model; Hydra-matic was offered for the first time.

LEFT The last LaSalle model year was 1940, when this Series 52 Special Coupe was made. Provided by Paul Shinnerer.

BELOW The first Cadillac 60 Special, introduced for 1938, was a highly individual design but remained in production for only four seasons. This car, provided by Alan Ravitch, dates from the final year, 1941, after which the Series 60 Specials began to lose their distinctive lines and look like other Cadillacs.

New lines and a new power unit

The V8 configuration was central to Cadillac thinking and the new unit, introduced for the marque's 1936 model year, gave all the smoothness and torque that had made each successive model the leader of its class. The gorgeous 45-degree ohv V12 and V16 had served their purpose, and production was now down to token quantities only. Simple logic said that the days were done for such engines. After all, the new V8 could outperform the V12 and match the V16. It may have seemed a retrograde step but, for 1938, engineer-in-chief Ernest Seaholm came in convincingly with a completely new, second generation, V16 engine exclusive to Cadillac. Based upon the new V8, this V16 had an included angle of 135 degrees. Its banks of cylinders would, therefore, be spread wider than before; but this did not matter, since the messages from Harley Earl's Styling Section were that bodywork was likely never to get any narrower.

Harley Earl's young protégé, Bill Mitchell, was the man who began this subtle change, or so it would seem from the work of art that first brought him rave reviews. Up to now, the running board had been integral to everyday car design. The typical American car was tall and wide, and elegant access dictated something to stand upon en route. By 1938, long and low lines were every designer's dream and, suddenly, the proximity of seat to ground level was being noted. Why *have* a running board at all?

Harley Earl was by now spending more of his time in the realms of fantasy, producing ideas for the future. His so-called Buick Y-job of 1937 anticipated a whole generation of imitation sports cars which would lead nowhere in the sports car domain; but it did provide suggestions for the ringing of model year changes. The Y-job did not have running boards; nor did Mitchell's 1938 Cadillac 60 Special: a new, compact four-light sedan combining artistic discipline with originality and instant customer appeal. It could be called the first of the modern Cadillacs. It may well have been the death of the LaSalle.

The Cadillac 60 Special did start a new concept: of that there is no doubt. For two or three seasons modern production methods had forced the stylist's hand, resulting in excessive roundness of line in the American car – especially in window, roof, and fender. However, Mitchell's first Cadillac combined curves and straight lines with – initially anyway – a lack of excessive ornamentation. The trunk was built in as an essential part of the integrated look. Although nicely rounded at the corners, all the 60 Special's windows had a flat base, which ensured a proper belt or waistline. The half-frame doors meant that the car had a sensible glass area, too.

The 60 Special had the easier-to-build monobloc V8 engine, by now two years old, and in its first year it was the best-selling Cadillac of all. However, 1938 was to prove a recession year, with car sales across the board diving again.

The end of the LaSalle, and of "traditional" Cadillacs
This recession was a brief one; 1940 would prove better, and 1941 would be a record. General Motors exceeded 2.3 million vehicle sales and the flagship, Cadillac, surpassed 60,000. (Up to that time, combined Cadillac-LaSalle sales had exceeded 40,000 units in only three calendar years: 1928, 1937 and 1940.) From 1942, LaSalle would no longer be a contributor to the Cadillac total. In yet another arbitrary move – and who is to say it was wrong? – LaSalle was eliminated from the GM program, just as shorter-lived companion marques had been ditched before it. In

LaSalle's case more hearts were broken, for this automobile had retained its personality to the very end. This was a time of reckoning, however, with famous independent names going to the wall or, if they were lucky, hanging on by the skin of their teeth with the promise of war contracts.

Since 1932 Ford had been establishing the V8 engine as an inspiration to all. Not only that, there was now a middle-price marque, the Mercury, as well as two new Lincoln V12 ranges: the Zephyr (with streamlining which succeeded, where that of the Chrysler-DeSoto had failed) and the Continental. With Packard, too, continuing to sell to a wider cross section of the public through reputation as well as quality, General Motors acted swiftly: Cadillac was now a world name, so why sell it under any other?

The Cadillac Series 62 Convertible Sedan (four-door drophead), one of only four hundred 1941 cars of this type built. Provided by Gordon Collins.

The final, 1940 series of LaSalles had their headlights mounted into the fenders but kept the high grille. With over 24,000 built, this year rated second only to 1937 in the marque's 14-year history: a history that could so easily have continued into modern times. The 1941 LaSalle was ready for announcement when it was axed. Harley Earl called several of his team's later dream cars "LaSalle," and these led to a GM competitor for the Ford Thunderbird; that competitor would, however, finally emerge as the 1963 Buick Riviera. Even in recent times, LaSalle has resurfaced, being shortlisted for a new, compact Cadillac. We shall meet it in a later chapter. But instead of LaSalle, it would be called Seville. Since Cadillac itself had been in danger of disappearing, the loss of LaSalle was, perhaps, a small price to pay.

The year 1940 was also the last for the fabulous V16, the model whose existence kept Cadillac exclusivity alive; but the day of true mass production, even for the best of automobiles, was at hand.

Only 61 Cadillac Series 90 (i.e. side-valve) V16s were built as 1940 models. There were still 11 different basic V16 body variations, from the regular $5140 sedan to the $7175 seven-seater town car. (The price of that year's most popular Cadillac, the 60 Special, was $2090.) The 1940 V16 was the last of the traditional Cadillacs: in future, Cadillac would have to fight harder than ever to maintain its observed superiority.

For the excellent 1941 and foreshortened 1942 seasons, Cadillac replaced its LaSalle with the Series 61, starting as low as $1345 for a 1941 coupe. Cadillac Hydra-matic automatic transmission, air conditioning and other luxuries became available with the Cadillac name before civilian production ceased.

44

The World War 2 years

Although war contracts had begun for GM in 1940, it was not until the attack on Pearl Harbor (December 1941) that America became completely committed to participation in World War 2. The making of cars for public sale ceased in early 1942 and would not restart until the late summer of 1945.

Cadillac's strength, and that of GM's other arms, was down to the management of Alfred Sloan. He had presided over GM from 1923 to 1937, seeing it safely through the world's worst modern business crisis. Then Chevrolet's chief executive William S. Knudsen had been appointed President, with Sloan becoming Chairman of the Corporation Board, and in 1940 they had celebrated the manufacture of GM's 25 millionth automobile: symbolically a Chevrolet, since that division had

Production of civilian cars ended in February 1942, shortly after this Series 67 Imperial Sedan was completed, not to resume again until late summer 1945. This rare example had done fewer than 50,000 (mostly chauffeur-driven) miles when provided for photography by Ed Cholakian.

become the biggest single producer in the world. There had been a human touch in the heavily self-congratulatory party atmosphere: a quietly smiling, neatly dressed figure was led to the platform. He and Alfred Sloan shook hands warmly. Between them they had created a remarkable empire. William Durant was then in his eightieth year, and chasing a new dream in the bowling alley business. He had been declared bankrupt a few years earlier but was now on a GM pension, which was no less than the creator of the Corporation deserved.

45

FINS AND FANTASY

*I*t was natural that, after the war, Europe should take much longer than the United States to return to normal. Even so, there was an appreciable delay before America's new automobile boom got under way, for its industry had its own problems, not the least of which was the shortage of steel and other basic materials.

There were only 16 major American marques by this time and 12 of them belonged to the "Big Three" corporations: General Motors, Ford, and Chrysler. The others would merge in the 1950s: Hudson with Nash to form American Motors; Packard with Studebaker to eventual oblivion (but not without a strong fight from some fine Raymond Loewy-styled cars on the way).

In 1945, however, came word of a new combine: Kaiser and Frazer. These cars named after Joseph A. Frazer and Henry J. Kaiser – one an automobile industry man, the other a millionaire public works contractor and wartime shipbuilder – seem to have acted as catalysts for the rest of the industry. The opportunism was exemplary: skilled people were looking for jobs; newly vacated factory space was going a-begging; and, across the United States and beyond, a whole new, mobile peacetime world was opening up. The Kaiser-Frazer Corporation was formed in August 1945 and by the end of 1946 it had produced close on 12,000 cars. Annual output nudged 140,000 units in 1947 and Kaiser-Frazer managed to average more than 100,000 cars per year until 1951. There followed a rapid downward spiral to rock bottom. With so many great names already gone, it had taken a special upstart confidence to create this brand-new pair of American marques which, in 1947, accounted for over 4 percent of US output. That put Kaiser-Frazer temporarily in fourth place, ahead of Studebaker, Nash, Hudson, and Packard. On the other hand, the "Big Three" still produced over 80 percent of North America's 3.5 million new cars. This was how the 1947 proportions looked:

General Motors 40 percent; Ford and Chrysler 21 percent each; Kaiser-Frazer 4 percent; Studebaker 3½ percent; Nash 3 percent (plus), Hudson 3 percent (minus); and Packard 1½ percent. Packard's share – less than 60,000 cars – was, in fact, comparable to that of its great rival Cadillac. Without a big corporation to back it, however, Packard, which outsold Cadillac in 1948 and 1949, had to go "down market" to survive. True, there was to be a special award from the New York Fashion Academy for Packard's 1948 styling; but too few customers liked this attempt to keep up with the moderns. There were several "special editions," which dented Cadillac's sales charts slightly, but from 1950 Cadillac always had the upper hand.

As in Chrysler's later efforts to reenter exclusive territory, Ford's luxury Lincoln lived with Cadillac but was never a threat to its existence. Indeed, Lincoln's switch from V12 to V8 engines – plus the option of Hydra-matic transmission (purchased from General Motors) from 1949 – could be

PREVIOUS PAGES Harley Earl's final fin, as seen on a 1959 Series 62 provided by Russ Barton (see also pages 62 and 63).

CADILLAC		
Series 62 Club Coupe		
1947		

ENGINE		**VEHICLE**	
Type	90° V, in-line, water-cooled	**Transmission**	Manual or Hydra-matic gearbox
No. of cylinders	8	**Driving wheels**	Rear
Bore/stroke	3.5 × 4.5 in (89 × 114 mm)	**Length**	215 in (5450 mm)
Displacement	346 cu in (5676 cc)	**Wheelbase**	129 in (3280 mm)
Valve operation	Side	**Weight (approx.)**	4000 lb (1820 kg)
Compression ratio	7.0:1	**Final drive**	Hypoid bevel
Carburation	One downdraft carburetor	**Suspension – front**	Independent
BHP	150 gross at 3400 rpm	**Suspension – rear**	Rigid
		Brakes	Drum

NOTES
Final season of pre-tailfin styling. This body
type also described as "sedanet."

ABOVE 1947 Series 62 Coupe (or Sedanet) shows the bullet-shaped fenders first featured for the 1942 season. Car provided by Ed Cholakian.

LEFT From 1948 the front fender line was carried through to merge with the rear one. This attractive 1948 Sedan, a Series 60 Special and another car from the Ed Cholakian collection, illustrates the first, subtle, use of the tailfin.

regarded as a straightforward compliment to the Cadillac concept of a top line car's ideal specification. General Motors had not been first with automatic transmission, but the Hydra-matic's experimental forerunner was already in hand with Cadillac engineers as early as 1934. There had been semiautomatic transmissions for Buick and Oldsmobile in 1937; and again it was the Oldsmobile Division that, from October 1939, offered the Hydra-matic as a production option, Cadillac following suit in the fall of 1940 for its 1941 model range. By now, therefore, GM had a clear lead in the field of automatics for all. Between them, Cadillac and Oldsmobile tended to remain GM's innovators: for example, both were to come out with new, high-compression, overhead-valve power units for 1949. These independently devised engines had "oversquare" dimensions – that is to say, the bore was greater than the stroke – and took Cadillac into the reawakening automobile racing arena, although this had not been GM's policy, as we shall see.

The 1948 range and the nascent fin

Cadillac's postwar production and sales were already soaring when the legendary 1948 range appeared. Strangely enough, the very distinctive shape and purity of line of the original 60 Special had been discarded after only four seasons (1938 through 1941) and for the curtailed 1942 season an unusual and bulbous podlike fender line was featured across almost the entire range. The exception was at the formal end of the spectrum: no longer the style-setting end. (In fact, the prewar Fleetwood 75 shape was kept right through to 1949. The name Fleetwood was, and still is, attached to this series, in honor of the once-famous body

49

company, long since lost within Fisher's customizing department.) One reason for the change in the 60 Special was, no doubt, related to the updating of body/chassis manufacturing techniques. Whatever the reason, the 1942-47 Cadillacs, except for an attractive fastback two-door coupe, did seem retrograde. On the 1947 catalog the caption "A New Standard of the World" appeared. This seemed less clear as a claim than Leland's original "Standard of the World."

The year 1948 was another period of innovation in the Cadillac styling studio, where William Mitchell was in charge – but only under the childlike gaze and godlike authority of Harley Earl, whose artistic

brilliance of the early 1930s had been replaced by a passion for gimmickry with aeronautical overtones. Although GM's central figure, Alfred Sloan, was still very much in command, other great names such as Dreystadt, Kettering, and Knudsen were no longer to be found. Earl, however, was only fifty-five years old and adding to his personal standing annually. He also fitted the Sloan requirement of catering for a market that was about to reach new record heights as the whole of America took to the road once again.

A 1952 example of the Series 60 Special, with the new feature of power-assisted steering, typifies the early development of Cadillac tailfin styling. Provided by Tracy Sheffield.

In Europe, the American idea of style in the 1950s – as led by Cadillac – was sneered at by some people, who believed that "fate" played an important part in automobile design. Others unashamedly copied "Americanisms," although few of these "translated" to the smaller scale of European cars with any success. The fact is that Earl and the folk of the GM divisional styling studios below him could dictate fashion at a time when everyone wanted to buy and the industry could not supply.

Other stylists did exist and they made their mark. In the summer of 1946, Howard A. Darrin introduced the straight-through fender line for Kaiser-Frazer, and Raymond Loewy the wraparound rear window for Studebaker. Then, in late 1947, came Frank Spring's remarkable new creation for Hudson ("The Car You Step Down Into"), surely the modern epitome of the "longest 'n' lowest" theory which Harley Earl had propounded for so long. It was GM that forced the pace next, and the basic shape of the new 1948 "Futuramic" Cadillac and Oldsmobile (to be adapted for Buick, Chevrolet and Pontiac in 1949) was outstanding in its original form, bearing much of the poise and elegance of the original Cadillac 60 Special of a decade earlier. (The coupe or sedanet version was certainly an inspiration for the 1952 Bentley Continental.)

Unfortunately, leaving well alone has rarely proved a good marketing policy; nor did it ever fit in with GM's annual-model-change thinking. And there was another thing: the continual need to differentiate between the five GM marques, and to keep Cadillac high on its pedestal. The 1948 answer to that problem would take Cadillac down a long, dead-end path – the path cleaved by the Harley Earl tailfin.

The concavity of the rear fender line, sweeping upward to the taillight cluster, should have sounded warning bells, but did not.

The fin effect, inspired by the twin-boom Lockheed P38 warplane, was inoffensive initially. Improved supplies of chromium meant that the eye

ABOVE Miles and Sam Collier shared the wheel of this Series 61 Coupe to finish a creditable 10th at Le Mans in 1950. Steady progress was made throughout the race, to the amazement of all. The entrant was the great and very popular American sportsman, Briggs Swift Cunningham.

BELOW Le Manstre in action at Le Mans in 1950, patron Briggs Cunningham at the wheel. With Phil Walters ("Ted Tappett") co-driving, he came 11th; the car's gearing was such that its special bodywork provided little advantage.

of the beholder was being drawn year by year to other embellishments such as Buick's LaSalle-inspired "portholes," and Cadillac's rear fender "air intake" (a dummy) of 1950. The fin was, however, unique to Cadillac at this stage and it caught on. While annual US car production went up from 5 to over 6 million at the turn of the decade, Cadillac quantities were moving rapidly through 90,000 and past the 100,000 mark, taking the luxury car theme forward to an era in which class consciousness was to be spelled out in carefully gradated block capitals.

Power and performance

The coming era was also to be one of high performance, unhampered by environmental legislation and heralded in America by the modern V8 engine. In Europe, special-purpose chassis were commonplace; powerful mass-production engines, though, were not. In the 1930s and 1940s several makes of Anglo-American hybrids had become popular with the sporting motorist. One of these, the Allard, was about to achieve world fame, thanks to the Cadillac engine.

The 1949 Cadillac V8 had been a well-kept secret, perhaps because it had had such a long gestation period while the side-valve unit continued to give sterling service. The development of this docile, compact, lightweight – 700 lb (320kg) dry – quiet, and relatively economical engine had been well advanced even before American industry switched to war work. Ernest Seaholm had seen it into being in the early 1940s, but as a complete project it was chiefly the responsibility of Harry Barr, John Gordon and Edward Cole: and the extent of its proving was prodigious. In original production form its power output was quoted as 160 bhp gross

Le Mans that year was the Russian-born Alec Ulmann. He was planning to bring endurance racing to the United States – a plan that would reach fruition with the birth of the Sebring series.

While in France, Ulmann had a long conversation with Raymond Acat, competitions secretary of l'Automobile Club de l'Ouest, the governing body for Le Mans, to establish just what kind of cars were being encouraged to take part. As a result of their experiences and discussions Chinetti and Ulmann were to play a part in instigating an even greater American involvement in Le Mans, starting with Briggs Cunningham's remarkable effort in 1950.

Shortly after that 1949 Le Mans race, Donald Healey introduced his new competition two-seater impressively: he and Ian Appleyard (having a rare break from Jaguar, his new XK120 not being ready) were close runners-up in the French Alpine Trial. Then, in August 1949, came the first-ever production car race at the new airfield circuit of Silverstone in Northamptonshire. Here the new Jaguars had their impressive one-two debut with Warwick-built Healeys fourth and sixth, sandwiched by three Frazer Nashes. It was from these performances that the Healey Silverstone got its name. Briggs Cunningham's purchase of one of these cars shortly afterward was followed almost immediately by the replacement of its 150 cu in (2.4-liter) Riley engine with a 331 cu in (5.4-liter) Cadillac: a transplant with a sequel.

Eighth and ninth in this parade of British sporting cars, and somewhat outpaced, came another brand-new competition machine, the Allard J2. Allard of Clapham, London, was still using outdated side-valve Ford V8s from Dagenham, the frustration being eased only slightly by the option of

LEFT Cadillac's ohv 5.4-liter V8 engine enabled sports car maker Sydney Allard of London and some of his customers to achieve international success in racing and rallying. This 1952 Allard J2X was a development of the J2 type with which Tom Cole and Sydney Allard had come 3rd at Le Mans in 1950.

(133 net) at 3800 rpm; yet it was reported at the time that "no appreciable wear" had taken place after one such engine had completed 100 hours of full throttle running at 4250 rpm; moreover, it was claimed that more than a million miles of running had been undertaken prior to public announcement.

Quite late in the program, the swept volume was increased from 309 cu in (5.06 liters) to 331 cu in (5.4 liters), simply to be one up on Oldsmobile which was known to be introducing its 304 cu in (5-liter) ohv Rocket V8 almost simultaneously. Such independence within a well-established group helps to emphasize the fact that a certain interdivisional autonomy – competitiveness even – was encouraged by GM's top brass. It is interesting to note that Jaguar's new long-stroke six-cylinder 200 cu in (3.4-liter) double-ohc XK engine also developed 160 bhp gross in touring form, but revolved quicker at 5000 rpm. The oversquare Cadillac engine had bore and stroke dimensions of 3.81 in (97 mm) and 3.63 in (92 mm) respectively, and Ed Cole specified that any compression between 7 to 1 and 12 to 1 should be viable.

The new V8 achieved its goals from the start and, suddenly, the Cadillac was not only America's fastest regular production car, but it found itself in the then exclusive 100 mph (160 km/h) class some two years before the appearance of Jaguar's first major dollar earner, the Mark VII of 1951.

Competition successes

For international motor racing 1949 was a revival year, and the Grand Prix d'Endurance at Le Mans was back on the calendar for the first time in a decade. Quite often in the history of the 24-hour-long classic, there had been a North American presence. In 1949, a New York-domiciled Italian, Luigi Chinetti, did most of the driving of the winning Ferrari. Also visiting

the "Ardun" Mercury overhead-valve conversion created by Zora Arkus-Duntov, later of General Motors. Import barriers kept the Cadillac engine out of Britain initially: but there was nothing to stop Sydney Allard selling his J2 chassis to the United States, less engine. The first of these was shipped out for Larry Kulok in August; the second, which went in October, was destined for the wealthy and enterprising young racing driver Tom Cole (no relation of GM's Ed Cole).

The first race of 1950 took place on the rain-soaked, wind-lashed streets of Palm Beach Shores, Florida, on January 3. Briggs Cunningham came second in the Cadillac-powered Healey, beaten only by George Huntoon in a Duesenberg-based former Indianapolis car. Tom Cole gave the Allard-Cadillac its first outing in the same event, starting well but failing (for reasons unspecified) to maintain the pace.

At about this time, through Tom Cole, Sydney Allard was able to obtain a Cadillac "development" engine, and this was installed in the prototype J2 in time for April's Targa Florio, a tough, traditional road race in Sicily. Allard and his loyal confidant, Tom Lush, survived several lurid half-accidents and near misses before the car caught fire. Anxious to save the new V8, they filled the engine bay with roadmen's gravel for protection. Fortunately the fire was confined to the rear of the car.

Meanwhile, Tom Cole's Allard-Cadillac was achieving success with a first and a close second at Westhampton, Long Island, in May. Early in June, Cole gave the Cadillac-powered Allard its first major win by taking the "feature" race at Bridgehampton, Long Island, from Sam Collier in Briggs Cunningham's Ferrari and Huntoon in the Duesenberg Special.

Immediately afterward, Tom Cole removed the dual-carburetor manifold from his car and made for the airport, whence he managed to carry the special assembly to London as "cabin baggage." Le Mans was only two weeks away and an entry had been secured for himself and Sydney

Allard. Upon Cole's arrival in London, the works Allard-Cadillac was fitted with the modification and dispatched to France.

First practice revealed a detonation problem with the engine, caused by the very low octane rating of Le Mans fuel. Three pistons were damaged and the only replacements in GM's Paris depot were oversize, so the cylinder block had to be rebored. This was achieved just in time for final practice, during which the engine ran well.

A surprise at Le Mans

The Allard was not the only Cadillac-powered machine to line up in echelon for the start of the 1950 Le Mans 24-hour race, for Briggs Cunningham was mounting an all-American Le Mans challenge.

Cunningham's first move had been to buy a "Fordillac" from its makers: Frick Tappett Motors Inc. of Freeport on Long Island. "Ted

The 1953 Cadillac Eldorado was priced at $7750 compared with $4150 for the more practical Series 62 Convertible it was based on. Just 532 of these "special editions" were built for that model year, by which time total Cadillac production was averaging well over 100,000 units per year. This "Eldo" provided by Carl Riggins.

Tappett" was the name used by Phil Walters as a midget car track racer; his partner William Frick was an ingenious special builder, and the "Fordillac" was a most effective and popular machine – the straight-forward installation of Cadillac's V8 engine in the latest Ford. Frick also engineered the Cadillac-powered Healey Silverstone for Cunningham, who was exploring every avenue to achieve his particular American dream. A Le Mans invitation had been received, thanks to Chinetti and Ulmann, but the Fordillac was not an acceptable entry. Donald Healey had by now completed a deal with Nash chief George Mason: so the only definitive "American" Healey was to be Nash-powered. On the other hand, the Frick Tappett Motors concern could now offer its own 220 bhp version of the Cadillac engine, known as the FT-390. So Briggs Cunningham bought two of the latest Cadillac Series 61 coupes and sent them to Freeport for preparation. One of them was to be driven, "city gent" style, by Miles Collier and his brother Sam, who described the car as "stock, except for Frank Burrell's efficient two-carburetor manifold, some air scoops welded to the brake drums, a 35-gallon extra gas tank in the trunk, conventional transmission instead of Hydra-matic, and race requirements such as hood straps, etc."

The other Cadillac had been delivered early enough for Frick Tappett

to turn it into a Le Mans "Special." Bodywork regulations being liberal, Phil Walters and Howard Weinman of the neighboring Grumman aircraft company got together and produced a distinctive but distinctly weird lightweight alloy body, which was laid over an aircraft-type tubular frame – in effect, a simplified form of the Italian *superleggera* technique. This, in the event, turned out to be of no particular advantage, due to the limitations imposed by regular gearing and a maximum of 4700 rpm even for the Frick-modified four-carburetor engine; but it was, certainly, an eyecatcher, and deserved its punning nickname of *Le Manstre*. Its looks were not helped by Phil Walters when, during a public relations exercise (namely that of taking Raymond Acat's secretary for a ride around the circuit before official practice) he managed to run it into a farmer's cart at a speed that was high enough to cause considerable damage to both machines but, happily, not to horses or human beings. A top body man was needed urgently, and America's best was holidaying in Britain. Briggs Cunningham, who brought a large support team to Le Mans, never did things by halves: Robert Blake and his wife were located and an aircraft was chartered to bring them both from England to France. Bob Blake stitched *Le Manstre* together expertly and became a member of the Cunningham team from then on.

stowed out of sight. Its trend-setting feature was the wraparound windshield – an aircraft cockpit motif adapted for the automobile. Only 532 of these Eldorados were made, carrying a $7750 price tag – twice the cost of a typical Cadillac. Alongside the new compact, sporting Chevrolet Corvette, however, the Eldorado looked gross. Cadillac was approaching its least-appealing period.

In 1954 all Cadillacs adopted the panoramic windshield, and the rest of the industry followed suit in an almost sheeplike way. It was difficult enough to compete with GM at the best of times. The "wraparound" disease would get worse before it got better and, all the while, the driver's knees and vision were being impeded quite seriously. The fact remains that Cadillac sales boomed, moving up inexorably from 100,000 toward 150,000 a year. With neither Chrysler (Imperial) nor Ford's Lincoln division fighting too hard, Cadillac reigned unchallenged over the luxury market of the 1950s.

The Big Three producers were now in a power war, all using modern V8 engines of great size and torque. Packard joined the V8 brigade for a final fling in this twilight world; but for that particular great marque the end was in sight.

Sheer size was not yet an embarrassment on the American motoring scene, and the automobile got lower, longer, and wider. In 1955, the Eldorado, not now such an exclusive type, more an earning member of the Cadillac family, showed the way to the tailfin's next stage of evolution. At first – and first is often best – there was an elegance in the elongation of the rear fenders; but in 1956 they were given a new upsweep, and the convertible (now called the Eldorado Biarritz) was joined by the first of the Eldorado hardtop coupes, dubbed Seville. Engine displacement went up from 331 cu in (5.4 liters) to 365 cu in (6 liters) giving the now-famous V8 engine a top rating of 305 bhp gross.

Flights of fantasy

A new substructure permitted 1957's Cadillacs to be even lower, and the frame design was one that permitted relatively cheap changes of wheelbase. Fresh flights of garish fantasy were reached in 1957 with the most exotic Eldorado of them all: the $13,000 Cadillac Fleetwood Eldorado Brougham hardtop sedan. (In Britain this would be a "pillar-less four-door.") Four headlights, heavy use of stainless steel and cockatoo color schemes hid a fascinating technical specification which included truck-type self-adjusting suspension by compressed air. This system was most effective – but only in principle, for it tended to leak. Every great marque has "off" days; owners of air-sprung Broughams would experience more of them than average. Seven hundred were made in two years. The more orthodox models were extremely reliable: a feature traceable back to the earliest precepts of Cadillac integrity in

Awkwardness of door line, caused by the modish wraparound windshield, is seen clearly on this heavily decorated 1958 Cadillac Eldorado Biarritz Convertible. The fins still had a year's growth ahead. Car provided by Gerard J. De Persio.

ABOVE AND RIGHT At $5450, the 1959 Series 62 Convertible offered better value than the $13,000 Eldorado Brougham (which, by now, was being made in Italy). This Series 62 illustrates the ultimate development of the multicurve windshield and the "space age" tailfin, after which Harley Earl bowed out to make way for more restrained stylists. Provided by Russ Barton.

BELOW By the 1960s, the dream theme was outdated. This sleek six-light Fleetwood 60 Special Sedan is marked as a 1964 model by its vestigial fins. The sensible windshield pillars had been restored a year earlier, just a decade after the introduction of the first Eldorado. It was a welcome return.

manufacturing; the marque's solidly founded reputation thus stayed intact. A noteworthy footnote to the Eldorado Brougham story is that, at his 1955 Motorama, Harley Earl had shown two dream cars called LaSalle II. One had been an open two-seater, the other a pillarless hardtop sedan from which the 1957 Eldorado Brougham format was derived. The name LaSalle vanished as quickly as it had reappeared, however. The idea of a one-horse carriage from the land of plenty must have seemed more appropriate at the time.

Even fewer of the 1959-60 Eldorado Broughams – two hundred or so – were produced. They were powered by a 390 cu in (6.4-liter) engine for which 345 bhp at 4800 rpm was quoted. They also had a European element in that they were finished not by Fleetwood but by Pinin Farina. They still possessed the unreasonably large tailfins of the day, but they did also represent a positive return to the harmony of line that had been lost since the arrival of the wraparound windshield. The screen pillar was slender and nicely angled, and it set the scene for a gradual toning down of the clamoring Cadillac forms of the '50s.

RIGHT The rise and fall of the fin: from 1948 through 1964, the Cadillac automobile was characterized by its distinctive tailfin. Inspired by the Lockheed P-38 aircraft, it began as a neat styling touch. It got out of hand in the late 1950s, however, and from 1960 the fin began to shrink, as did the amount of chromium plate applied. By 1965 the fin had vanished altogether (see pages 64-65).

CADILLAC
Fleetwood Eldorado
1965

ENGINE

Type	90° V, in-line, water-cooled
No. of cylinders	8
Bore/stroke	4.1 × 4 in (105 × 102 mm)
Displacement	429 cu in (7031 cc)
Valve operation	Overhead
Compression ratio	10.5:1
Carburation	One four-barrel carburetor
BHP	340 gross at 4600 rpm

VEHICLE

Transmission	Hydra-matic three-speed gearbox
Driving wheels	Rear
Length	224 in (5680 mm)
Wheelbase	130 in (3290 mm)
Weight (approx.)	4660 lb (2115 kg)
Steering	Power assistance standard
Suspension – front	Independent
Suspension – rear	Rigid
Brakes	Drum

NOTES
New perimeter frame permitted all 1965 Cadillacs to have engine mounted 6 in further forward.

This 1965 Fleetwood Eldorado Convertible, provided by Ed Berry, cost $6600 when new. The Fleetwood name is kept alive even today, in honor of the bodymaking house that was integrated with GM's Fisher so many years ago.

Into the 1960s

Harley Earl retired in 1959 (the year of the biggest fins of all) although he would remain in the design consultancy business for the remaining decade of his life. He had brought "art and color" (or styling) to the automobile in its most commercial form, and was a major influence on the strength of General Motors. He never gave up his quest for lowness and length in the car, and it was his successor, William Mitchell, who had the task of turning the GM model range toward a less ostentatious future, without loss of sales, or disturbance of a marque "pecking order" with Cadillac at the top.

There was nothing unusual about interchange of ideas with Europe. Chrysler and Ghia were very close, as was Farina with Cadillac.

So Cadillac entered the 1960s in more sober mood. Although the Farina car and the Seville were gone by 1961, the Eldorado Biarritz convertible and the rest of the range took on a more orthodox look. Fins came down; pillars, rooflines and lamp surrounds were squared off; and for 1965 a new perimeter-type subframe was adopted. As usual, however, the Fleetwood Seventy-Five (Cadillac's formal car) was left until last. Eventually, for 1966, it acquired a particular handsomeness which, ironically, made that year's Cadillac range the sleekest – as Earl would have wanted – as well as the tidiest-looking since the war.

More than 200,000 Cadillacs were made in 1966: a record, but one that would be beaten many times as Cadillac surged ahead into another new age of luxury motoring.

SMALLER CARS, BIGGER BUSINESS

During the 1960s, General Motors' other car divisions produced many imaginative designs and, for a time, it seemed as if the Cadillac would become a dinosaur. The compact Chevrolet Corvair, although sadly out of date in today's terms was, in 1960, a brilliant combination of Ed Cole engineering and Bill Mitchell styling. That car did not deserve the notoriety singled out for it by "safety" campaigner Ralph Nader.

Other Mitchell triumphs of the decade included the 1963 Sting Ray version of the Chevrolet Corvette and GM's answer to the second-generation Ford Thunderbird: the Buick Riviera, a personal sports coupe which had started out as another abortive LaSalle revival. The Mitchell team emphasized its professional capabilities yet again in 1966-67 with the Chevrolet Camaro and Pontiac Firebird, the neoclassic "Ponycars": so-called in deference to Lee Iacocca's Ford Mustang, the car that was succeeding where the poor Corvair had failed – in the new sporting compact market.

For 1966 – the year in which Alfred Sloan, GM's Honorary Chairman died, aged over ninety – Oldsmobile was selected to set another ball rolling, with the spectacular Toronado. In 1967 a similar mechanical layout was offered by Cadillac for a completely new edition of the Fleetwood Eldorado coupe. This was not a case of playing second fiddle to anyone – more one of Cadillac taking time to refine an excellent concept, and using it to recreate an identifiable supercar. Yet the price, $6300, kept it within sight of the cheapest ($5000) Cadillacs, by now known as the Calais series.

The 1967 Fleetwood Eldorado coupe was everything the Eldorado Brougham of a decade earlier should have been. It was big, yet it was beautiful; it had well-proved advanced features such as ventilated disk brakes at the front and – most significantly – front-wheel drive. These, together with the sophisticated suspension incorporating torsion bars at the front, gave Cadillac a new technical superiority within the US automobile industry. The styling was another magnificent exercise in automobile sculpture, and few, if any, better-looking *big* American cars have been introduced subsequently. A particularly clever Eldorado exercise in packaging was to install the Hydra-matic transmission unit beneath one of the cylinder banks, alongside the block. From the torque converter, behind the engine crankshaft, a flexible drive provided the transmission link.

Emission control: the Cadillac response

In 1968 came the first full year of emission control regulations. This, and the new safety legislation, would influence the world's industry, forcing designers to think with more imagination – in new directions.

Initially, the tendency was to enlarge engine capacities to offset the power loss. Cadillac was no exception. For 1968 a 472 cu in (7.75-liter) V8 was introduced. Two years later it would be supplemented by a 500 cu in (8.2-liter) unit with a nominal power rating of 400 bhp at 4400 rpm; perhaps the 1970 Eldorado's "8.2-liter" badge was intended to emphasize the fact that this was the world's biggest road-car engine. (This engine was still listed as recently as 1976, by which time its output had fallen to a quoted maximum gross bhp of 190 at 3600 rpm.)

The new front-wheel-drive Eldorado was soon selling at a rate of over 20,000 units a year, while the total annual Cadillac output was constantly above 200,000. The market was still there; then came the oil producers' embargo and a short-term panic, affecting 1974 particularly. Sales during the late 1970s would carry Cadillac past the 300,000 units per year mark, increasing the domestic share from (in general terms) 2 to 3 percent over the decade.

This dramatic success was not just a function of Cadillac's near monopoly of the luxury sector; rather, it was a result of the survival battle, in an age when the large American car (as typified by Cadillac) would become outmoded. Cadillac had the answer: it would bring down the scale – but not the prestige *or* the price! There would be big, orthodox Cadillacs, as well as the front-drive Eldorado; but they would be supplemented by a new "international-sized" car.

Attack from abroad: the Seville defense

By the mid-1970s, the competition from imported luxury cars was becoming acute. BMW, Mercedes-Benz, Volvo and Jaguar were determined to take advantage of the situation, and the Cadillac response (after

PREVIOUS PAGES From 1986, the compact front-drive V8 Eldorado illustrated shared with the Seville many structural and mechanical features as Cadillac broadened its horizons to stay competitive.

BELOW Most significant of all Eldorado models was the clean-lined 1967 Coupe, its styling being William Mitchell's responsibility. The landmark feature of this car, however, was the use of front-wheel drive. Provided by Vern Brown.

CADILLAC Eldorado Coupe 1967	
ENGINE	
Type	90° V, in-line, water-cooled
No. of cylinders	8
Bore/stroke	4.1 × 4 in (105 × 102 mm)
Displacement	429 cu in (7031 cc)
Valve operation	Overhead
Compression ratio	10.5:1
Carburation	One four-barrel carburetor
BHP	340 gross at 4600 rpm
VEHICLE	
Transmission	Hydra-matic three-speed gearbox
Driving wheels	Front
Length	221 in (5610 mm)
Wheelbase	120 in (3050 mm)
Weight (approx.)	4850 lb (2200 kg)
Steering	Varying ratio
Suspension – front	Independent
Suspension – rear	Rigid
Brakes	Drum
NOTES	
Disk brakes at front, optional this year, would become standard shortly.	

the 1973-74 "crisis") was quick and clever. Cadillac's first "compact," announced as a 1976 model as early as April 1975, had "European" proportions and distinct Rolls-Royce and Mercedes-Benz overtones in its smart, simple lines. At $12,500 it was the most expensive "personal" Cadillac: the Eldorado convertible was then listed at $11,000, and the Calais series at under $9000. (The 1976 Eldorado convertible would be the last Cadillac softtop for eight seasons. The Calais series was about to be dropped, too: but that was for marketing rather than potential legislative reasons which looked, for a time, as though they could force the total disappearance of the open car.)

For the newcomer the name LaSalle was, once again, dredged up only to be ditched. That marque had been discontinued over 30 years earlier, so perhaps there was little relevance in resurrecting it? "LaSalle" is on ice, however, and suggestions as to its re-use still crop up from time to time within GM. It was from the more recent past that the new Cadillac's name emerged. Between 1955 and 1960 a hardtop version of the Eldorado had been known as the Seville. Now, with Cordoba and Granada in use by the opposition, it was decided to give that evocative geographical name back to Cadillac for its most significant announcement in years.

A Convertible Eldorado supplemented
the fixed-head Coupe model from 1971.
This example, provided by Larry Moore,
Sr., dates from 1974 – the year in which
sales slumped so badly because of
the Middle East oil embargo.

The 1975-76 Seville looked right. Itt was 900 lb (400 kg) lighter, 8 in (200 mm) narrower and 27 in (700 mm) shorter than the most popular contemporary Cadillac – confusingly called the DeVille. It had an Olds-based 350 cu in (5.7-liter) V8 engine with electronic fuel injection (a feature that became optional on other Cadillacs). The first 2000 cars created the image that GM wanted; not too many potential customers could have owned one of those late-1930s 60 Specials, but Bill Mitchell was by now as famous as Harley Earl, and most Cadillac owners knew the legend of Mitchell's first masterpiece. Mitchell himself went on record as saying that he had tried to recapture the spirit of his first 60 Special in the new Seville. The fascinating part of the story is that history did, in a way repeat itself. The first 60 Special had kept its original purity of line for just four model years before changing in character. Now, the same thing would happen with the Seville. In a sense, however, the brand-new Seville for the 1980 season was a styling reprise.

At the 1948 London motor show, the first one there after World War 2, self-expression abounded as the British industry struggled toward distant prosperity. The great makers, like Rolls-Royce and Daimler, were still relying on traditional bodywork – often commissioned by the individual customer, or created speculatively for display (a ploy that America had taught the world). Several examples were exhibited by one of the most celebrated of all the long-established (by now Daimler-owned) specialists, Hooper & Co. of London, at that 1948 show. Most eye-catching was a "three-plus-two" of enormous size, fitted with power-operated convertible top; its body line was accentuated by the completely filled-in rear wheel arch (not such an uncommon thing) and a unique front fender line that swept through to the tail. This "Green Goddess" had no rear fender line at all: a Hooper hallmark in subsequent

CADILLAC
Eldorado Convertible
1976

ENGINE

Type	90° V, in-line, water-cooled
No. of cylinders	8
Bore/stroke	4.3 × 4.3 in (109 × 109 mm)
Displacement	500 cu in (8194 cc)
Valve operation	Overhead
Compression ratio	8.5:1
Carburation	One four-barrel carburetor
BHP	190 at 3600 rpm

VEHICLE

Transmission	Hydra-matic three-speed gearbox
Driving wheels	Front
Length	224 in (5690 mm)
Wheelbase	126 in (3210 mm)
Weight (approx.)	5290 lb (2400 kg)
Steering	Varying ratio
Suspension – front	Independent
Suspension – rear	Rigid
Brakes	Disk all round

NOTES

215 bhp EFI version also offered. (Final year of 8.2-liter engine.)

ABOVE The new Seville, introduced in 1975, might have been named the "Leland," or even "LaSalle"; undoubtedly it showed GM's determination to place its prestige marque firmly in the luxury compact class which was being dominated increasingly by imports. This 1976 Seville provided by Alan Ravitch.

CADILLAC
Seville Elegante
1980

ENGINE

Type	90° V, in-line, water-cooled
No. of cylinders	8 (*see* **Notes**)
Bore/stroke	4 × 3.4 in (103 × 86 mm)
Displacement	350 cu in (5737 cc)
Valve operation	Overhead
Compression ratio	8.0:1
Carburation	Electronic fuel injection
BHP	180 at 4400 rpm

VEHICLE

Transmission	Four-speed automatic, with overdrive
Driving wheels	Front
Length	206 in (5220 mm)
Wheelbase	114 in (2895 mm)
Weight (approx.)	3814 lb (1730 kg)
Steering	Recirculating ball
Suspension – front	Independent
Suspension – rear	Independent
Brakes	Disk all round

NOTES
Diesel versions of the 5.7-liter engine (plus 6-liter V8, 4.1-liter V6, and 4.1-liter V8 gasoline units) were also used for "second generation" Sevilles.

years. More artistically conceived was Hooper's Touring Limousine, which won the top coachwork award. Like the "Green Goddess," which inspired the famous "Docker" Daimler show cars, the Touring Limousine was built on the Daimler DE36 straight-8 chassis. It also had sculptured razor-edge lines that blended subtly, to merge at the tail. (This type was exhibited at the 1949 New York show, listed at $22,000!)

In 1968 – long after he had acquired Daimler on behalf of his company, Jaguar – Sir William Lyons unashamedly adopted these Hooper motifs for his own design of modern Daimler limousine replacement. (This model is still being made in small quantities by Jaguar at the time of writing.) Then, more than a decade later, Sir William was for once outdone when Cadillac's Wayne Cady reestablished the 1940s Hooper line for the 1980s. (Mitchell, who retired in 1977, had in fact overseen a Hooper-style mock-up earlier.) The exercise did work, and proved that there is room in any generation for a look at the past while designing for the future.

ABOVE Seville joined the front-drive tendency from 1980 with this distinctively restyled model, provided by A. Wolfe Motors. The shape, inspired by a British Hooper body design idiom first seen in the late 1940s, was to be discarded six seasons later.

RIGHT This 1984 Sedan DeVille ensured a continuing rear-drive presence within the Cadillac range; 1986 saw the succession pass to the Fleetwood Brougham, with promises from GM of more rear-drive cars to come – so long as the market dictates.

However, the 1980 Seville was not just a new-*look* Cadillac. The mechanical layout was transformed, too – and it showed clearly that Cadillac was heading down the front-drive route. It possessed four-wheel disk brakes (as later versions of the previous Seville had done) and independent suspension all round, plus yet more sophisticated engine and occupant management systems. Engine options varied yearly, as economy and low emission regulations grew tighter. There was a pioneering spirit in the creation of a V8 engine programmed to cut out the use of unnecessary gasoline-drinking cylinders; early faults were never overcome, however, and the "V8-6-4" was abandoned by the mid-1980s when the engine range for larger Cadillacs consisted of Cadillac's own 250 cu in (4.1-liter) V8 (new from 1982) and two Oldsmobile diesels, a 260 cu in (4.3-liter) V6 and a 350 cu in (5.7-liter) V8.

Now for the 1990s

By 1986 a third-generation Cadillac Seville had been launched, and it typified a whole new era for the American automobile. As in 1985, the Type HT 4100 250 cu in (4.1-liter) V8 gasoline engine with digital fuel injection was fitted as standard; the difference, now, was that the power pack was installed transversely under the hood rather than longitudinally. The compression ratio was 8.5 to 1 and the nominal net power output 130 bhp at 4200 rpm. The new layout was just one factor in a remarkable reduction in the vehicle's overall bulk. With the wheelbase reduced by 6 in (150 mm) and a shortening of the vehicle by 16 in plus (more than 400 mm), compared to the previous year's model, Cadillac's 1986 Seville showed the determination of Detroit to meet the threat of European and Japanese luxury compacts head-on. Moreover, the new Seville was 375 lb (over 170 kg) lighter than its immediate forebear and could show notably improved city and highway fuel consumption of 17 mpg (14.24 liters/100 km) and 26 mpg (9.31 liters/100 km).

The four-speed automatic transmission with overdrive was retained

for 1986, with the added attraction of a viscous converter clutch which, when engaged, reduced torque converter slip to a minimum through the coupling medium of a silicone fluid, as opposed to the more conventional steel spring damper. The 1986 Seville also featured completely revised independent suspension all round, by the MacPherson strut principle in front, and incorporating a fiberglass transverse spring at the rear. All-disk braking, already a Seville feature, was retained and, with rack-and-pinion steering to replace the recirculating ball type, the 1986 range looked surer footed than any previous Cadillac lineup.

The 1986 Seville was, therefore, in complete contrast to its immediate predecessor. Gone were the sweeping and distinctive (if controversial) lines, replaced by a businesslike boxiness; but it had luxury and advanced technology in abundance, too.

Remarkably similar to the four-door Seville was the 1986 version of the two-door Cadillac personal luxury coupe – the Eldorado. Close on 20 years had passed since the announcement of the original front-wheel-drive Cadillac, which also bore the Eldorado name. Now virtually every model in the range featured front drive, in complete contrast to the American scene of just a decade earlier.

Besides the brand-new Seville and Eldorado, the 1986 Cadillac Coupe, the Sedan DeVille and the front-drive Fleetwoods shared the same 250 cu in (4.1-liter) transversely mounted V8 power unit. There were smaller engines, too: 122 cu in (2-liter) 4-cylinder unit with electronic fuel injection and a multi-port 171 cu in (2.8-liter) V6 developing 85 and 120 bhp net respectively at 4800 rpm. These were for the smallest Cadillac of all. Not for over 65 years had a 4-cylinder Cadillac been offered when, in the early 1980s, the Cimarron was launched. This truly compact sedan was based on GM's world-famous J-car, known to the British as the Vauxhall Cavalier. The 4-cylinder engine did not give this car much appeal in America, so the V6 option was introduced in 1985 to justify GM's description of the car as a luxury sports sedan.

Tradition and continuity

From early 1986, the traditional rear-wheel drive V8 model, the Fleetwood Brougham, received a new lease of life: a 305 cu in (5-liter) V8 engine replacing the 250 cu in (4.1-liter) unit. At 221 in (5614 mm) the Fleetwood Brougham was considerably longer than the Fleetwood Seventy-Five limousine, which had changed its image from push to pull for the 1985 model year. The rear-wheel drive Fleetwood Brougham sedan and the special edition version known as the d'Elégance wore their years well; but even the most loyal of Cadillac customers could no longer live in the past, and by 1986 there was a new breed of potential Cadillac user among the younger high-flying executives to be found throughout the North American continent. The aim of GM's Cadillac Motor Car Division in the late 1980s and in the 1990s was to woo them.

Potentially the most significant modern Cadillac launch was that of a new 1987 model, the Allanté. As if acknowledging the inroads made by the great marques of Europe on the American scene, Cadillac's General Manager and GM Vice-President John Grettenberger introduced it as combining "the best of European design and specialty craftsmanship with state-of-the-art American production and engineering technology." His remark referred to Pininfarina's renewed involvement as designer and manufacturer of the two-seater convertible coupe's bodywork, and a

FOLLOWING PAGES Genuine leather continued to be an Eldorado feature, when this famous Cadillac name was applied to a truly compact Coupe for 1986. The engine was mounted transversely, but it was still a V8!

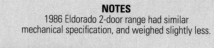

CADILLAC			
Seville			
1986			
ENGINE		**VEHICLE**	
Type	90° V, transverse, water-cooled	Transmission	Four-speed automatic, with overdrive
No. of cylinders	8	Driving wheels	Front
Bore/stroke	3.5 × 1.7 in (88 × 44 mm)	Length	188 in (4780 mm)
		Wheelbase	108 in (2743 mm)
Displacement	250 cu in (4087 cc)	Weight (approx.)	3428 lb (1555 kg)
Valve operation	Overhead	Steering	Rack & pinion
Compression ratio	8.5:1	Suspension – front	Independent
Carburation	Digital fuel injection	Suspension – rear	Independent
BHP	130 at 4200 rpm	Brakes	Disk all round

NOTES
1986 Eldorado 2-door range had similar
mechanical specification, and weighed slightly less.

LEFT The "third-generation" compact Seville epitomized the marque's 1986 character, with a V8 gasoline engine – a configuration originally used by Cadillac more than 70 years earlier – now mounted crosswise and, naturally, driving through the front wheels.

LEFT From 1985, even the long-established Fleetwood 75 Formal range incorporated front drive and transverse mounting of its V8 engine, heralding a new era for the American limousine.

RIGHT Launched in 1981, the Cimarron was the first 4-cylinder Cadillac to be offered for more than 65 years. Its performance potential was enhanced from 1985 by the option of a 171 cu in (2.8-liter) V6 engine.

plan to operate a thrice-weekly Alitalia-Lufthansa 747 "airbridge" carrying up to 56 units per westbound flight from Turin to Detroit. Build of an estimated 7000 Allantés per year will be completed at GM's Detroit-Hamtramck assembly center.

In the smaller car categories, GM and Japan – through Isuzu, Suzuki and Toyota connections in particular – were working closely together to make international vehicles. By 1986, however, despite its modernity and advanced technology, the Cadillac range retained a peculiarly national product identity. Many of the original Leland precepts lived on, too. For example, the completely new Eldorado/Seville range was being produced in the General Motors B-O-C Detroit-Hamtramck Assembly

Center where the modern equivalent of Leland's quality control system was installed. Claimed to have "the most thorough and extensive electrical check systems in the industry," Detroit-Hamtramck consisted of 77 air-conditioned acres (31 ha) containing more than 20 miles (32 km) of conveyor. Bodymaking, painting and vehicle assembly were undertaken in near clinical conditions with computers, laser cameras and other sophisticated equipment – vying with the encouragement of employee participation in maintaining the one traditional aspect of Cadillac to which GM's management remained committed: the quality factor that had led Cadillac's founder Henry Leland to proclaim one standard for all his products. He had called it Standard of the World.

INDEX

Acknowledgments

The publishers would like to thank the following individuals and organizations for their kind permission to reproduce the photographs in this book:

Peter Roberts (pages 8 left, 9 color and inset, 14 below, 18 above)
GM Photographic (pages 8 right, 13 above, 14 above and center, 24 above, 57 below, 62 below, 63 extreme right, 75 below, 78 below, 79 below)
Quadrant Picture Library (pages 10 all photographs, 34 above)
Topham Picture Library (page 19 below)
Louis Klemantaski (page 52 both photographs)
Neill Bruce (page 53)
Nicky Wright (pages 74-75 center)

All other photographs specially taken by:

John Lamm (endpapers, pages 1-5, 11-12, 13 below, 15-17, 19 above, 20-21, 25 above, 28-33, 35 above, 36-40, 46-47, 54-55, 56-57 above, 58-59, 62-63 above, 64-67, 72-73, 74 above, 76-77, 78-79 above)

Dennis Adler (pages 6-7, 18 below, 22-23, 24-25 below, 26-27, 34-35 below, 41-45, 48-49, 50-51, 60-61, 68-71)

The author and publishers would like to thank Norbert Bartos and Vicki Longwish of General Motors in Detroit, and Ken Moyes of General Motors UK, for their help in the preparation of this book. Many thanks, too, to the owners and custodians of the cars who kindly allowed their vehicles to be photographed.